EXECUTIVE SUMMARY

This paper is a study of over 900 biographies of the deceased militants of Lashkar-e-Taiba (LeT), a Pakistani militant group that has waged a campaign of asymmetric warfare against Indian security forces and civilians in the contested region of Kashmir for over two decades, as well as other parts of India more recently. Although LeT had a storied history on the eve of its high-profile November 2008 terrorist assault on the Indian city of Mumbai, that particular event and the case of American LeT operative David Headley (who conducted the reconnaissance for the attack) thrust the organization and the evolving threat it poses to regional security and Western interests into broader international consciousness. That attack, coupled with LeT's recruitment of Westerners and linkages to a number of other international terror plots over the past decade, have heightened concerns that the group's interests and operational priorities are no longer just regional, but that they are also becoming (or have already become) global. This has led to a proliferation of interest in LeT and a desire to learn more about the group's behavior and how it operates outside of the South Asia region.

Instead of evaluating evidence of the group's internationalism, as many recent studies have attempted to do, this study is more foundational in focus. It is predicated on the assumption that LeT's local activity and infrastructure are and will remain the key source of its strength, even if the group decides to become more active in the international arena. By leveraging biographical information extracted from four Urdu language publications produced by LeT from 1994 to 2007 and statistical information released by the government of Pakistan, this study aims to provide baseline data about LeT's local recruits, the nature of the time they spend with the group and how these dynamics have changed over time. Specific emphasis is placed on providing insights into the following four research questions:

1) What is the general background of LeT's local fighters?
2) How and from where are these fighters recruited?
3) What level of training do these fighters have and where were they trained?
4) Where exactly do LeT's fighters die?

A summary of our main findings and the some of the related implications follow.

Fighter Background

- <u>Age:</u> According to our data, the mean age when a recruit joins LeT is 16.95 years, while the militants' mean age at the time of their death is 21 years. The mean number of years between an LeT militant's entry and death is 5.14 years.

- <u>Family:</u> Siblings and parents are central characters in the biographies and they play important roles in a fighter's entry into and journey through LeT. For example, siblings or other immediate family members were often the one to drop off a LeT recruit at a training camp or at the border before his mission. This finding suggests that scholars should reconsider the value of parental influences in understanding radicalization and a young person's decision to participate in jihad.

- <u>Nonreligious and Religious Education:</u> The most common level of nonreligious education attained by LeT fighters (44 percent of available data) before their entry into the group is matric (tenth grade), indicating that on average the group's cadres had higher levels of secular education than other Pakistani males.

- According to our data, religious education supplemented nonreligious education for LeT recruits rather than the former serving as a substitute for the latter. The amount of time fighters spent at a madrassa was less than three years on average. Fewer than five percent of fighters on which we have this type of data attained a *sanad* (a formal certificate signifying completion of a defined religious curriculum), indicating that LeT fighters do not have high levels of formal religious education.

Residence and Recruitment

- <u>Location:</u> The vast majority of LeT's fighters are recruited from Pakistan's Punjab province. While LeT's recruitment is diversified across the north, central and southern parts of the Punjab, the highest concentration of LeT fighters have come (in order of frequency) from the districts of Gujranwala, Faisalabad, Lahore, Sheikhupura, Kasur, Sialkot, Bahawalnagar, Bahawalpur, Khanewal, and Multan.

- <u>Means of Recruitment:</u> Based upon our data, we identified twelve different channels of LeT recruitment, the most common forms of which include recruitment via: a current LeT member (20 percent), a family member (20 percent), mosque or madrassa (17 percent), LeT speech or literature (12 percent), and friends (5 percent).

Since 2000 there has been a strong upward trend in recruitment via family members and by 2004, this channel contributed to over 40 percent of LeT recruitment.

Training, Deployment and Death

- <u>Location and Level of Training:</u> LeT training has historically occurred in Muzaffarabad, Pakistan and in Afghanistan. Together these two locations have accounted for 75 percent of LeT militant training over time.

  The highest level of training reported by most LeT militants (62 percent of available data) was specialized training (*Daura-e-Khasa*, LeT's advanced course), the majority of which occurred in Muzaffarabad. An additional 12 percent of fighters were able to name other specific training courses, which potentially followed *Daura-e-Khasa*.

- <u>Fighting Fronts and Location of Death:</u> Ninety four percent of fighters list Indian Kashmir as a fighting front. Although less relevant, Afghanistan, Chechnya, Tajikistan and Bosnia are also identified in the biographies as other fronts.

  According to our data, the districts of Kupwara, Baramulla and Poonch in Indian Kashmir account for almost half of all LeT militant deaths since 1989. Kupwara, the district with the largest number of militants killed, appears to be becoming less important overall as a fighting area, with its share of deaths declining over time. The number and share of LeT deaths in Baramulla and Poonch have been increasing. LeT fighter deaths in Indian Kashmir have also become more geographically distributed over time, suggesting that the group has intentionally pursued this type of strategy or is responding to pressure applied—or new campaigns waged—by Indian security services in select districts.

Implications

There are a number of important implications associated with this research. First, given that our data provides insight into high-density areas of LeT recruitment and the specific recruitment methods employed by the organization in those locales, it can be used by relevant planners to enhance strategic communication and other Counter Violent Extremism initiatives in Pakistan. Second, this paper and the associated data can be used as a foundation for academics and counterterrorism practitioners to build upon and to better understand LeT's local activity and how it has evolved over time.

INTRODUCTION

The presence of U.S. and international troops in Afghanistan since October 2001 have been a visible and seductive target for a broad range of local and foreign militants that represent a multiplicity of agendas. For some of these militant groups, the conflict in Afghanistan has functioned as an opportunity—and also potentially as a distraction. While the number of insurgent attacks in Afghanistan has generally risen since 2008[1] (with seasonal ebbs and flows and yearly fluctuations), the level of militant-linked violence in Indian-administered Kashmir—the theater where many Pakistan-based groups have historically been active—has declined from levels seen during the late 1990s and early 2000s.[2] Once the primary battleground for jihad in South Asia; over the last decade the fight in Kashmir just hasn't been as relevant for jihadist actors.[3] If history and the area to which Pakistani militants (aided by the state) turned their operational attention after the Soviets departed Afghanistan is any guide,[4] the reduction of the U.S. footprint in Afghanistan in 2014 could help to change that. While it is difficult to predict the directional priorities of Pakistan-based militant groups after the United States reduces its role in Afghanistan, especially in light of the internal security challenges faced by Pakistan and the state's own shifting threat priorities, historical precedent suggests that some of these militant groups will reorient to and invest more broadly in the conflict in Kashmir.

The series of skirmishes between Pakistani and Indian forces along the Line of Control in Kashmir in January 2013, which resulted in the reported deaths of at least one Pakistani and two Indian soldiers (one of whom India claims was beheaded), have

---

[1] For background, see Ian S. Livingston and Michael O'Hanlon, "Afghanistan Index: Also Including Selected Data on Pakistan," (Washington, DC: Brookings Institution, 13 December 2012), 10.

[2] Shushant K. Singh, "Indian Kashmir Steps Away from Violence," *World Politics Review* (31 May 2011), www.worldpoliticsreview.com/articles/9007/Indian Kashmir-steps-away-from-violence; Sandeep Joshi, "Marked Decline in Terrorist Violence in J&K, Says Prime Minister," *The Hindu*, 8 September 2012, www.thehindu.com/news/national/marked-decline-in-terrorist-violence-in-jk-says-pm/article3874146.ece.

[3] "Annual Fatalities in Terrorist Violence in Terrorist Related Violence 1988–2013," South Asia Terrorism Portal, undated, www.satp.org/satporgtp/countries/india/states/jandk/data_sheets/annual_casualties.htm.

[4] For background on Pakistan's historical support for Islamic militants both before and after the anti-Soviet jihad see C. Christine Fair, "The Militant Challenge in Pakistan," *Asia Policy* 11 (January 2011), 105–137; for other general dynamics see Sumit Ganguly, "Explaining the Kashmir Insurgency: Political Mobilization and Institutional Decay," *International Security* 21, no. 6 (Fall 1996), 76-107.

1

brought the potential for renewed conflict in Kashmir into sharp relief.[5] This has left many regional observers trying to discern whether this incident was isolated or a harbinger of more violence to come between two nuclear-armed neighbors who have fought three conventional wars since 1947. Should elements of Pakistan's security establishment view it in their interest to spoil peace or reignite conflict in the region (potentially to serve as a release valve for domestic challenges or to redirect the actions of militants actively waging war against Islamabad), they will likely turn to trusted Pakistani militant groups, such as Lashkar-e-Taiba (LeT), to do their bidding.

For the past two decades LeT has steadily emerged as one of Pakistan's most lethal and capable militant proxy groups. Its long-term approach and the scale and scope of its activities, which largely revolve around efforts to conduct *da`wa* (missionary activism), to reform Pakistani society from within, and to engage in violent external jihad, especially in India, have helped the group develop a domestic political constituency and gain international reach.[6] While the group has historically been used by Islamabad as an agent of regional foreign policy—and one that has been mostly focused on waging a low-level war of attrition in Indian Kashmir—a steady array of incidents tied to the group over the last decade strongly suggest that LeT's interests are evolving and that its operations in the future might be less constrained. The November 2008 terrorist attacks in Mumbai, India, serve as an important case in point, as this attack demonstrated the group's capacity for innovation and its ability to execute and tactically manage from afar complex, multistage operations against a mix of regional and international targets—and to do so in dramatic form, and in a media-savvy way.[7] That the reconnaissance for this operation and another plot against the Danish newspaper that published the cartoons of the Prophet Muhammad in 2005 was conducted by an American citizen (David Headley) from Chicago has further heightened concerns, leaving some to question whether Mumbai was an outlier or a sign of a broader

---

[5] Jason Burke and Jon Boone, "India and Pakistan Trade Accusations after Kashmir Border Skirmishes," *Guardian*, 10 January 2013, www.guardian.co.uk/world/2013/jan/10/india-pakistan-kashmir-border-skirmishes; "India says Pakistan 'beheaded' Kashmir soldier," BBC News, 9 January 2013, www.bbc.co.uk/news/world-asia-india-20954975.

[6] For general background on LeT see Stephen Tankel, *Storming the World Stage: The Story of Lashkar-e-Taiba* (New York: Columbia University Press, 2011).

[7] For background see "A Perfect Terrorist," *PBS Frontline*/ProPublica, 22 November 2011, www.pbs.org/wgbh/pages/frontline/david-headley/.

strategic or ideological shift taking place within the group, with more, similar international attacks to come.[8]

Western counterterrorism investigators have been particularly troubled by LeT's recent attack history, its links to several international terror plots, the group's transnational footprint, the accessibility of its infrastructure in Pakistan and the two-decade-long spillover associated with its training camps. The group's active recruitment of U.S. and European citizens and the discovery of a number of LeT operatives and cells based in both places have led some researchers to conclude that a threat to the U.S. homeland by this organization (or an associated splinter group or LeT-trained element) can no longer be ruled out.[9] Even if this is not the case and the group maintains a more limited operational focus on Kashmir and India in the years to come, its attack on Mumbai raises the specter that future attacks orchestrated by the group in that region may be more hybrid in nature or international in flavor—helping LeT to draw world media attention to its cause. Due to these dynamics, it is imperative that the academic, policy, law enforcement and intelligence communities forge a better understanding of how LeT operates in the region and what this group does and with what local human capital.

Despite the prominence and enduring presence of LeT in Pakistan, there have been few efforts to collect data on its activists and, in turn, to develop more useful insights into the group's cadres and recruitment practices. This lacuna is surprising given that the organization has produced and continues to produce massive amounts of materials about itself and its cadres that are available in the public domain, albeit mostly in Urdu. This report leverages some of this material and aims to close this gap by exploring four questions about the group's members:

---

[8] Ibid.

[9] For U.S. examples see the cases of David Headley and Tahawwur Rana; see also Jerry Markon, "Final Defendant Guilty in 'Va. Jihad'," *Washington Post*, 7 June 2006, www.washingtonpost.com/wp-dyn/content/article/2006/06/06/AR2006060601142.html; "Maryland Man Sentenced to 15 Years for Providing Materiel Support to Terrorist Organization," PR NewsWire, www.prnewswire.com/news-releases/maryland-man-sentenced-to-15-years-for-providing-material-support-to-terrorist-organization-52771312.html; Carol Cratty, "Pakistani sentenced to 12 years for aiding terror group," CNN, 13 April 2012, www.cnn.com/2012/04/13/us/virginia-terror-sentencing/index.html; for examples of LeT recruiting other westerners see the story of Charles Wardle in Sebastian Rotella, "The American Behind India's 9/11—And How U.S. Botched Chances to Stop Him," ProPublica, 24 January 2013, www.propublica.org/article/david-headley-homegrown-terrorist; and "'Australia Terror Plotter' Jailed," BBC, 15 March 2007, http://news.bbc.co.uk/2/hi/europe/6454373.stm.

1) What is the general background of LeT's local fighters?
2) How and from where are these fighters recruited?
3) What level of training do these fighters have and where were they trained?
4) Where exactly do LeT's fighters die?

To provide insight into these questions, the research team acquired a collection of biographies of LeT fighters published in several different Urdu-language publications produced by the group over a fifteen-year period. After studying the obituaries of these killed militants, the team then coded and statistically assessed details relevant to the four questions above. We sought to evaluate these data in relation to other published work on LeT and militant recruitment in Pakistan and, when possible, to statistical information produced by the government of Pakistan. Despite the limitations of the data that we employ, we hope that this work serves as an important, foundational step forward toward understanding how local recruits in Pakistan enter and spend time with LeT.

A description of our data and the important caveats with which researchers must approach them is provided next, and it is followed by a brief discussion about the relevance of this report and its findings. The report is then organized topically in line with the four questions above. It concludes with a brief discussion of the strategic implications of this research effort.

DATA AND METHODS

Our data set includes biographical information and other key details about 917 LeT militants killed from 1989 to 2008. The biographies reviewed for this report were derived from four primary sources in Urdu published by LeT. One hundred and eighty biographical records were coded from a three-volume book, *Hum Ma'en Lashkar-e-Taiba Ki* (*We, the Mothers of Lashkar-e-Taiba*), which was edited and in part authored by Umm-e-Hammad; 14 records were coded from *Majallah Taibaat* (*Journal of Virtuous Women*);

4

696 records from *Majallah al-Dawa (Journal for the Call to Islam)*; and 27 from *Mahanah Zarb-e-Taiba (Monthly Strike of the Righteous)*.[10]

Empirically, such a sample suffers from selection bias in ways that we are unable to identify. Even though we made every effort to acquire as many records as possible, we cannot say how representative this resulting sample is of all LeT recruits generally. Thus for purposes of analysis, we must treat this sample as a nonrepresentative sample, as we are unable to specify the universe from which it is drawn and thus compare the characteristics of this sample of LeT activists to the entire unobserved population of LeT cadres. It should be stated clearly that while this nonrandomness of the sample precludes us from generalizing to the entire organization, it is likely impossible ever to know the entire universe of LeT activists, much less the entire pool of persons from which LeT recruits. However, we have attempted where possible to compare our sample of LeT recruits to other data about Pakistani males more generally from Pakistan's Bureau of Statistics. This at least allows us to demonstrate the differences between our sample and Pakistani males at large.

The biographies' formats vary, ranging from short pieces with minimal information to longer and more detailed biographies that are several pages in length. Overall, the biographies reflect the outlook of LeT more than that of the individual. The format of the biographies in *We, the Mothers of Lashkar-e-Taiba*, is, for example, mostly consistent,

---

[10] *Majallah al-Dawa* (renamed *Al-Haramain*) has been Laskhar-e-Taiba's and Jamaat ud-Dawa's (JuD, LeT's sister organization) most important publication over time. The first issue of the magazine was published in March 1989. It is edited by Maulana Amir Hamza, the founding ideologue of the JuD. Qazi Kashif Niaz is also believed to have been an editor of *al-Dawa* for a certain period of time. Typically, every issue carries articles on what being a Muslim should mean to every Muslim, especially from the Ahl-e-Hadith school of Islamic jurisprudence. *Al-Dawa* also usually carries reports of jihad (particularly in Indian-administered Kashmir), information about fallen militants and updates about the workings of all JuD departments. *Al-Dawa* reportedly has a circulation of 140,000. Other LeT linked magazines include: *Ghazwa Times* (renamed *Jarrar*), *Taibaat* (a bi-monthly magazine for women, which has been renamed *Al-Saffat*), *Voice of Islam* (an English-language magazine, which has been discontinued), *Nanhe Mujahid* (a monthly now released under the name *Rozatul Atfal*) and *Al-Ribat* (a monthly magazine in Arabic, which is now branded as *Al-Anfal*). Umm-e-Hammad is the compiler of the three-volume series *Hum Ma'en Lashkar-e Taiba Ki*; the editor of LeT's magazine for women, *Taibaat*; the head of LeT's women's wing; and a mother to two LeT martyrs. For background see C. M. Naim, "The Mothers of the Lashkar," *Outlook India* (15 December 2008), www.outlookindia.com/article.aspx?239238 and Humeira Iqtidar, *Secularizing Islamists: Jama'at-e-Islami and Jamat'at-ud-Da'wa in Urban Pakistan*, (Chicago: University of Chicago, 2011), 106–107.

and begins with the militant's alias name, followed by a description of his background and personal story, brief battle details and a will.[11] The biographies from the three other LeT publications follow a similar format.

The dominance of the organization's voice is reflected in the repetition of tone, perspective, attitude, writing style and the religious justifications used. The most consistent element in the biographies is the *wasiyatnama*, or will, of the militants, which indicates that LeT may provide militants with a standard template to fill out before their operational deployment.[12]

Data Extraction

Construction of this database began as an iterative process, and it was designed to complement similar data-driven efforts conducted by scholars interested in the background and behavior of militants from other regional areas.[13] We identified several personal characteristics that were highly desirable for our study and would provide insight into the background, recruitment, training and deployment of LeT fighters. These characteristics specifically include the militant's age, place of origin, level of secular and religious education, length and type of militant training (and the location of that training), deployment area, place of death, means of recruitment and any available family details. Our primary data analyst drew a random sample of our biographies to determine whether these or other data elements were generally available for most of the biographies. She determined that often these elements were available. In some instances, she found that biographies contained information about family background (e.g., marital status, numbers of siblings, parental status and the like). However, such details were usually rare.

---

[11] For a debate on the authorship of *We, the Mothers of Lashkar-e-Taiba* see C. M. Naim, "The Mothers of the Lashkar," *Outlook India* (15 December 2008), www.outlookindia.com/article.aspx?239238.

[12] In addition to paying tribute to LeT's fallen fighters, the publications served at least four other purposes: 1) to honor the families 2) to cultivate and retain ideological, social, or financial support for LeT 3) to recruit new members and 4) to communicate the message, purpose and achievements of the group as part of its messaging strategy.

[13] For example, see Appendix 1 in Thomas Hegghammer, *Jihad in Saudi Arabia: Violence and Pan-Islamism since 1979*, (Cambridge: Cambridge University Press, 2010). The authors would like to thank Thomas for sharing additional information about his data set on Saudi militants.

Once we established the list of data elements that we wished to extract, we drafted a code book to guide data extraction and replicability. (A list and explanation of the variables that were coded can be found in Appendix A and the full Data Appendix that accompanies this paper.) The desired data elements were then extracted from the biographies and translated, then categorized and recorded using Microsoft Excel. For each record, our data analyst detailed the source of the biography as well as all the information available in each biography. As with all data extraction exercises, this often involves making judgment calls, which is unavoidable. For example, a biography may not specify the number of years of education attained by a militant. Instead, the biography may simply say that the individual was a "graduate." At the appropriate places below and in the appendices, we describe the categories that we employed and the judgment that coding entailed.

Clearly this is an imperfect process. Whereas it would be desirable to have multiple coders and then generate statistics on the degree to which they agreed or disagreed in coding (inter-rater reliability statistics), in this exercise we had one coder. Finding multiple coders who were proficient in Urdu, who had an understanding of the group in question and who had experience in data collection proved extremely difficult. Thus the data set that results reflects the systematic judgment of one coder.

Data Caveats

While our data set is large compared with similar studies, several caveats must be kept in mind. First, while we attempted to acquire a complete set of each of the LeT magazines reviewed to ensure consistency of our data, some gaps in our collection remain. For example, we do not have every issue of each magazine published during the period of our study even though we have coded every magazine we could acquire (see Appendix B for the list of all LeT magazines incorporated into this data set). Second, as noted above, there is no way of knowing how representative these militants are relative to all of LeT's cadres. Our review of the biographies reveals that, in many cases, the fighters described here had to consistently lobby the organization for additional training and for eventual deployment. Clearly not everyone recruited by LeT ends up fighting in theatre (i.e. in a conflict zone like Indian Kashmir). It is therefore not possible to say how representative our fighters are relative to all of LeT's cadres, especially those fighters who did not die, and we cannot say anything about how they compare with the entire pool of persons who wanted to join LeT but who were not selected or deployed by the organization. Thus, while it is still possible to compare the attributes of our fighters to the society from which they are drawn, one should be cautioned against making sweeping conclusions about the ballast of LeT's members based on this data alone.

Further, while still useful as a source, there are problems associated with studying militant propaganda. All of the coded biographies in our data set were extracted from publications produced by LeT, and thus the view presented in these biographies represents the view that LeT—or the editor of each respective publication—intentionally wanted to communicate to the public. Due to a number of constraints, the research team was not able to interview fighters' families or to corroborate the stories of the fallen militants that show up in our data set. It is our hope that other researchers with better access to local communities in the Punjab and elsewhere throughout Pakistan will augment this dataset with interviews from the field.

IMPLICATIONS

Counter Violent Extremism Programming

Some of the obvious implications of this work pertain to Counter Violent Extremism (CVE) programming in Pakistan, which is one of the central goals of the Pakistan Communications and Engagement Plan, adopted by Secretary of State Hillary Clinton and approved by President Obama in 2010. As Marc Grossman, the U.S. Special Representative to Afghanistan and Pakistan, explained in Islamabad in April 2012,

> We have a strong interest in the stability and prosperity of Pakistan and the
> region, including a secure, stable, prosperous Afghanistan, and [in putting] an
> end to the safehavens and enablers on both sides that allow violent extremists
> to threaten both of our peoples. We have a common enemy and a common
> cause. . . . [There] is joint work to do to defeat terrorism and to defeat violent

extremism. As Secretary Clinton recently said, there needs to be a coordinated and concerted effort to combat extremists of all kinds. . .[14]

Effective programming to diminish the support that LeT enjoys and to degrade their ability to recruit, raise funds and operate effectively in Pakistan and abroad requires a more informed understanding of who joins LeT, the specific locations where they are from and the nature of the time they spend with the group.

Our analysis of these biographies casts considerable light on why individuals join LeT. In general, LeT fighters viewed association with the group as a means to live a more meaningful or purposeful life. Some were specifically motivated by corruption in their societies, others by what they saw as moral depravity that is inappropriate for a Muslim state.[15] Some articulated a moral obligation to help fellow Muslims who experienced oppression and even death at the hands of non-Muslims, particularly in Indian Kashmir, as their motivation to join the organization.[16] Others were moved by images of mosques being destroyed or Qur'ans burned.[17] Unfortunately, due to these dynamics, it will be challenging for the United States to affect these sources of motivation.

Family dynamics were found to be an important driver of militant recruitment and may present important opportunities for CVE programming. Mariam Abou Zahab's own analysis of LeT biographies led her to a similar conclusion about the importance of mothers in particular. She found that militants were highly solicitous of their mothers'

---

[14] U.S. Department of State, "Marc Grossman and Jalil Abbas Jilani, Joint Press Availability" (April 26, 2012), http://islamabad.usembassy.gov/pr_42612.html.

[15] For general background on LeT fighter motivations, see Farhat Haq, "Militarism and Motherhood: The Women of the Lashkar-i-Tayyibia in Pakistan," *Signs: Journal of Women in Culture and Society* 32, no. 4, (2007), 1039; on petty corruption, see the biography of Muhammad Akhtar (alias Abu Qatada) in Umm-e-Hammad, *Hum Ma'en Lashkar-e-Taiba Ki*, vol 1 (Lahore: Dar ul-Andalus, 1998), 50–54; on moral depravity, see the biography of Muhammad Arshad (alias Abu Hataf) in *Majallah al-Dawa*, June 1996, 8.

[16] Political violence did not figure prominently, if at all, in the biographies. Yet it is political violence in Indian Kashmir and the actions of security forces there that ironically justifies the narrative for many of these young men to join the organization. For an example see Umm-e-Hammad, *Hum Ma'en Lashkar-e Taiba Ki*, vol. 2 (Lahore: Dar ul-Andalus, 2003), 47.

[17] For example, one of the militants expressed his desire to take revenge for the destruction of the Babri Masjid (the Mosque of Babur) in India's Uttar Pradesh as one of his reasons for joining LeT (see the biography of Abu Sanaullah Qazzafi Butt in *Majallah al-Dawa*, August 1997).

blessing for their activities.[18] Siblings too play an important role in either enabling or discouraging a young man's ultimate decision.[19] These findings suggest that terrorism scholars should think about recruitment as a decision influenced by family dynamics as well as individual and other processes.

This insight suggests a critical area of future inquiry should data exist or become available: the role of family members in the decisions of aspiring activists who ultimately relent either in their decision to join LeT or to embark on an operational mission. The importance of family should not be a surprise. After all, many of these young men are teenagers when they are recruited. While the U. S. military allows recruits to sign up when they are seventeen, their parents must agree to this decision. Thus, even for U.S. military recruiters, the recruitment of young persons can often be a family affair.[20] In many cases, LeT activists had friends and family members who were in the organization already, and a select number of LeT activists were related to the group's senior leaders.[21] This too is similar to traditional military recruitment patterns in which friends and families play an important role in the recruitment of the individual.[22] Refocusing efforts upon what makes some families and other influencers

---

[18] Mariam Abou Zahab, "I shall be waiting for you at the door of paradise," in *The Practice of War: Production, Reproduction and the Communication of Armed Violence*, Aparna Rao, Michael Bollig and Monika Bock, eds. (New York: Berghahn Books), 133–158.

[19] A survey of the families of militant fighters in Pakistan, previously conducted by one of the authors, reached a similar conclusion about the role played by family members. For background see Victor Asal, C. Christine Fair and Stephen Shellman, "Consenting to a Child's Decision to Join a Jihad: Insights from a Survey of Militant Families in Pakistan," *Studies in Conflict and Terrorism*, 31, no. 11 (November 2008), 1003–1005, 1011.

[20] Scott Conroy, "Army Enlistment Becomes Family Affair," CBS News, 11 February 2009, http://www.cbsnews.com/2100-201_162-1913741.html. Also see "Joining—A Family Decision," undated, www.goarmy.com/soldier-life.html. There could also be cultural reasons or related explanations as to why we see family playing such a strong role in LeT recruitment.

[21] For example, see the biography of Abu Hanzala Zahid—a relative of Hafez Saeed (his grandmother was the leader's sister)—who worked for Zaki ur-Rehman Lakhvi in LeT's accounting office before his death. (*Mothers*, Vol III, 91-96). Another militant, Abu Bakr Siddiq Cheema, was the nephew of the LeT leader Hafez Abdul Raheem Cheema (*Majallah al-Dawa*, February 1996, pp. 17-18), while yet another was the nephew of Markaz al-Dawa's administrator, Abdul Majeed (*Majallah al-Dawa*, July 1996,. 8—10). One of the sons of Umm-e-Hammad also shows up in our data set. (*Majallah al-Dawa*, July 2000, 20). Other militants were similarly related to several LeT leaders through family and marriage. See, for example, the biography of Abu Hafs Khalid Waleed (*Mothers*, Vol I, pp. 334-336).

[22] See extensive discussion about influencers in U.S. Army, *Recruiter Handbook*, USAREC Manual 3-01, 22 November 2011, http://www.usarec.army.mil/im/formpub/rec_pubs/man3_01.pdf.

encourage jihadism while others discourage it may create new insights and opportunities for CVE programming in Pakistan.

Recruitment Base and Other Linkages

The Pakistan government insists that Pakistanis are not engaging in acts of terrorism in India or elsewhere; rather, the government claims that it is only providing diplomatic and moral support to the indigenous mujahidin fighting in India.[23] While few entertain these claims as credible, our database indicates that this claim is false. First, the vast majority of LeT fighters are Pakistani and most are Punjabi, not Kashmiri. It is noteworthy that there is considerable overlap among the districts that produce LeT militants and those that produce Pakistan army officers, a dynamic that raises a number of questions about potentially overlapping social networks between the army and LeT.[24] While certainly not the norm, at least eighteen biographies in our data set describe connections between LeT fighters and immediate family members (i.e., fathers or brothers) who were currently serving or had served in Pakistan's army or air force. In several of these cases, the militant's father had fought with the Pakistani army in the 1965 war in Kashmir (the Second Kashmir War) and/or during the conflict in 1971 over the status of then East Pakistan (since known as Bangladesh).[25] In one case a militant's father was described as a senior officer in the Pakistani army.[26]

---

[23] See Sultan Ahmed, "The terrible threat of terrorism," *Defence Journal* (February 2000), http://www.defencejournal.com/2000/feb/terrorism.htm, and "Pakistan to continue support to Kashmir cause: PM," *Siasat Daily*, 6 July 2012, www.siasat.com/english/news/pakistan-continue-support-kashmir-cause-pm.

[24] Compare the heat maps of LeT recruitment to those of the Pakistan army presented in C. Christine Fair and Shuja Nawaz, "The Changing Pakistan Army Officer Corps," *Journal of Strategic Studies* 34, no. 1 (February 2011), 63–94.

[25] For example, see the biography of Abu Tayyib Qari Muhammad Akbar (*Majallah al-Dawa*, August 1997, 17–19).

[26] See the biography of Abu Zarr Shams al-Arifain in *Majallah al-Dawa*, undated. It is also worth noting here that a number of LeT militants also had connections to elite Pakistani institutions and Pakistani religious leaders and politicians. Two that are noteworthy are that the uncle of one militant was a Director at Pakistan's Atomic Energy Commission (who is reported to have tried to dissuade the young fighter from joining LeT and to join the Army instead), while the father of another was the president of the Pakistan Muslim League's labor wing in Islamabad/Rawalpindi. For details see the biographies of Abdul Razzaq Abu Abdullah (*Mothers*, Vol II, pg. 38-50) and Abul Qasim Muhammad Asghar (*Majallah al-Dawa*, October 1997, pg. 26).

LeT draws in recruits using a variety of means, both through proactive targeting of potential cadres by LeT recruiters at schools, mosques and madrassas; as well as through LeT's extensive publication and office infrastructure throughout Pakistan.[27] Indeed, such expansive and overt presence throughout the country speaks to a degree of tolerance if not outright assistance from the Pakistani state. Equally notable is the fact that the vast majority of the fighters in this database died in Indian-administered Kashmir. This truth, taken with the predominantly Pakistani-Punjabi origins of the fighters, collectively puts to rest any of Pakistan's claims about the nature of its citizens and their activities.

The Madrassa Myth, Revisited

Pakistan's madrassas have been a focus of the policy community because of their alleged ties to producing terrorists since 2000, when Jessica Stern penned an article for *Foreign Affairs* in which she intimated that these seminaries are weapons of mass instruction.[28] Other scholars continued to link madrassas with terrorism,[29] despite the paucity of data for the linkage.[30] The biographies studied for this report indicate that on average LeT's cadres had higher levels of nonreligious education than Pakistani males —even relative to the Punjab, from which the vast majority of these cadres come.[31] This is true whether we compare them with rural or urban men across Pakistan generally or in the Punjab in particular.

---

[27] For more detailed background, see the recruitment section below.

[28] Jessica Stern, "Pakistan's Jihad Culture," *Foreign Affairs* 79, no. 6 (2000), 115–26; Jessica Stern, "Meeting with the Muj," *Bulletin of the Atomic Scientists* 57, no. 1 (January/February 2001), 42–50.

[29] "Pakistan: Madrassas, Extremism and the Military," *International Crisis Group (ICG) Asia Report*, 36, 29 July 2002; Peter Singer, "Pakistan's Madrassas: Ensuring a System of Education Not Jihad," Brookings Institution Analysis Paper, no. 14, November 2001.

[30] See C. Christine Fair, *The Madrassa Challenge: Militancy and Religious* Education (Washington D.C.: USIP), 1008; Peter Bergen and Swati Pandey, "The Madrasa Scapegoat," *Washington Quarterly* 29, no. 2 (Spring 2006), 117–125; Christopher Candland, "Religious Education and Violence in Pakistan," in *Pakistan 2005*, Charles H. Kennedy and Cynthia Botterton, eds. (Oxford: Oxford University Press, 2006), 230–255; and Alexander Evans, "Understanding Madrasahs," *Foreign Affairs* 85, no. 1 (January/February 2006), 9–16.

[31] The biographies of 454 fighters provided this type of data (49 percent of our total observations). For additional background see the Education subsection below.

It is also likely that for our militants, madrassa education was in addition to nonreligious education rather than a substitute for the same. For those militants for whom we have data about their length of religious education (a very small number), the average tenure at a religious school was 2.8 years.[32] However, very few of the militants in our data set actually attained a religious certificate (*sanad*).[33] At a minimum, it takes two years of study at a formal madrassa that teaches the *Dars-e-Nizami* curriculum to attain the first *sanad*.[34] This is consistent with militants spending relatively little time at a madrassa. Further, since LeT has a strong proselytization mission that aims to convert persons from other religious traditions (i.e., Barelvi) to the Ahl-e-Hadith interpretative tradition, it is possible that an individual fighter began his religious schooling *after* the recruitment process began. Indeed, our biographies provide evidence that this is the case. While we cannot determine when a recruit began religious schooling, we can say for certain that the vast majority of them also had relatively high degrees of secular education (as compared to Pakistanis on average) in addition to their religious training.

FIGHTER BACKGROUND

Despite the prominent role played by LeT in South Asian terrorism, little is actually known about the group's regular fighters. To address this gap, this section aims to provide insights into the sociological and personal characteristics of those who fight on behalf of LeT. It does so by specifically exploring the background of LeT fighters in relation to their age, family background, level of nonreligious and religious education, occupation and—where relevant—statistical information produced by the government

---

[32] Only 5.4 percent of biographies studied provided data about the length of religious education. As there are data on the average length of time that one spends at a madrassa in Pakistan, we have no way of benchmarking this to the nonmilitant population. Moreover, given that this information was so infrequently provided in our biographies, one should be cautious in interpreting this figure.

[33] See below for additional background on *sanad* and the different types.

[34] "Dars-i-Nizami: Curriculum devised by Mullah Nizamuddin Sihalvi (d.1748), a scholar in Islamic jurisprudence and philosophy based at Farangi Mahal (a famous madrassah in Lucknow).1 (Not the same curriculum propounded by Mullah Nasiruddin Tusi (d.1064) at the Nizamia madrassah he established in eleventh-century Baghdad. Almost all Sunni madaris—irrespective of whether their sectarian affiliation is Barelvi, Ahl-e-Hadith, Jamaat-i-Islami, or Deobandi—follow this course of study, formally adopted by the Deoband seminary in 1867. Shia madaris have a similar multiyear curriculum." C. Christine Fair, *The Madrassah Challenge*, USIP, 2008, xvii; A *sanad* certifies that an individual has undergone a religious curriculum or is trained and competent in a specific course, such as Qur'anic studies, *hadith* or Arabic. For additional details see Appendix D.

of Pakistan. However, the relevant data caveats must be kept in mind. These data are derived from our sample and do not represent all of LeT's cadres, much less the entire pool of persons aspiring to join LeT but were never selected.

Age

The mean age when a militant joins LeT is 16.95 years, with the median age being 16.5.[35] The youngest recruit in our data joined at the age of 11.5, while the oldest recruit was 30. Ninety percent of the militants joined LeT before they were 22 years old. The mean age of a new LeT enlistee corresponds to the age Pakistani students typically are about to finish their matric program (tenth grade).[36]

Militants' mean age at the time of their death in our data is 21 years, while the median age of death is 20 years.[37] The youngest militant whose death is recorded in our data is 14 years, while the oldest is 43 years. These findings are very similar to those found by one of our authors from a survey she conducted of 141 militant households in Pakistan.[38]

While our data sample is limited to only those fighters who died and whose death was highlighted by LeT, our data appear to show that militants do not live long after they have been recruited by the group. In our sample, the mean number of years between an LeT militant's entry and death is 5.14 years, and the median is 4.0 years.

---

[35] We define joining LeT as the age when the militant either was recruited into the organization or carried out basic training. We have this type of data for 68 individuals (7.4 percent of our total pool of 917 biographies).

[36] Pakistan follows a 10+2 educational system, where a student is considered to be matric passed after successfully completing tenth grade examinations, and intermediate passed after twelfth grade.

[37] For this variable, we have data for 235 fighters (26 percent of our total data).

[38] Christine Fair and her team specifically found that "for the 124 *shaheeds* [martyrs] for whom we obtained age of death of data, the youngest was 12 years and the oldest was 52 years of age. The average and median age of death was 22 years of age. The bulk of these fighters (79%) died between the ages of 17 and 25." See C. Christine Fair, "The Educated Militants of Pakistan: Implications for Pakistan's Domestic Security," *Contemporary South Asia* 16:1 (March 2008), 98. A breakdown of the militant groups associated with the sample are provided on page 99 of that same study.

Family Dynamics

Marriage and Children

It is likely that a majority of militants are not married nor have children, since these family members were not discussed in a majority of the biographies (17.1 percent of the observations provided data for this field, and only 55 LeT fighters noted that they were currently married while 99 stated they were unmarried).[39] In several cases, mothers attempted to prevent their sons from fighting by trying to persuade them to marry.[40]

Siblings

Siblings are central characters in the biographies, and they play important roles. For example, in several cases siblings supported (i.e., provided permission) and opposed their brother's decision to fight.[41] Siblings or other immediate family members were also often the one to drop off a LeT recruit at a training camp or at the border before his mission.[42] According to the biographies, after the death of the militant, siblings occasionally provided continuing support for the organization through financial means and sometimes with promises to fight as jihadists themselves.[43] This finding is

---

[39] Two additional LeT fighters had been married previously but were divorced, and thus we decided to not include them as they were not married at the time of their death. Also, even though a large percentage of militants used or were given a *kunya* that incorporated "Abu" (which would normally indicate that the fighter was a father), the research team only coded the fighter as having children if this was explicitly stated in the biography. For general background on LeT's use of this *kunya* see Mariam Abou Zahab and Olivier Roy, *Islamist Networks: The Afghan-Pakistan Connection* (New York: Columbia University Press: 2006), 39.

[40] Mothers of LeT militants interviewed by Farhat Haq noted their employment of the same approach: "She was worried that he [her son] would go back to the [LeT] training camp and thus was planning a quick wedding for him as a strategy to keep him home. This woman was not alone in resisting LeT's jihadi mission for her son." See Farhat Haq, "Militarism and Motherhood," 1043.

[41] We also coded the number of siblings in our data set. Where siblings were mentioned, the militants' families had an average of 2.69 brothers and 2.04 sisters per household. According to the 1998 census, the average household size in Pakistan was 6.8 (6.8 for rural households and 7.0 for urban.) If one assumes a two-parent household, then these LeT households are not out of the ordinary. See Pakistan Census Organization, Pakistan Census 1998, "Population by Sex, Sex Ratio, Average Household Size and Growth Rate," www.census.gov.pk/populationsex.htm.

[42] For examples see the cases of Abu Sultan Muhammad Abdullah (*Majallah al-Dawa*, June 2000) and Abu Khabeeb Habeeb ur Rahman (*Mothers*, Vol I).

[43] For examples see *Majallah al-Dawa*, June 2001, page 41; *Majallah al-Dawa*, July 2001, page 47; *Majallah al-Dawa*, July 2001, page 54.

important because the general literature on radicalization and participation in terrorist groups tends to exclude family dynamics as key variables of study.

Mothers

Parents are also an important part of the biographies. Mothers, for example, serve as the primary lens through which the biographies found in the three-volume series *We, the Mothers of Lashkar-e-Taiba* are told. The author-editor of those publications, Umm-e Hammad, is herself the mother of a fallen LeT fighter (in addition to being the head of LeT's women's wing).[44] In that series, the role of women is relegated to traditional roles, and mothers are portrayed as their Muslim ideal, a paragon of religiosity: one who is sacrificial, patient and grateful.[45] Mothers are supporters, but they are secondary to the paramount position of young men and the LeT. Farhat Haq notes that, "Although women are not given military training, many of the women leaders are taken to the training camp to witness the training of young men."[46] This finding too suggests that scholars should reconsider the value of parental influences in understanding radicalization and a young person's decision to participate in violent extremist organizations.

Education

There is a lingering belief in the policy community that Islamist terrorists are the product of low or no education or are produced in Pakistan's madrassas, despite the evolving body of work that undermines these connections in some measure.[47] Our work on LeT continues to cast doubt upon these conventional wisdoms. As we demonstrate in the following section, LeT militants are actually rather well educated compared with

---

[44] For debates on Umm-e-Hammad's role and the potential role played by others in compiling this three-volume set see C. M. Naim, "The Mothers of the Lashkar"; for original source, see Umm-e-Hammad, *Hum Ma'en Lashkar-e Taiba Ki.* (Lahore: Dar ul-Andalus, 1998). For additional background on Umm-e-Hammad, see Farhat Haq, "Militarism and Motherhood," 1041–1042.

[45] For a rich treatment of the role of women within LeT, and the politics associated with how their role is presented in LeT's propaganda, see Farhat Haq, "Militarism and Motherhood," 1023–1046.

[46] Farhat Haq, "Militarism and Motherhood," 1030–1031.

[47] For a broad overview of some of this issue, see "Exploding misconceptions: alleviating poverty may not reduce terrorism but could make it less effective," *Economist* (16 December 2010), http://www.economist.com/node/17730424; C. Christine Fair, "The Enduring Madrassa Myth," *Current History* 111, no. 744 (April 2012), 135–140.

Pakistani males generally. This is an important contribution to the ongoing debate about the relationship between education and militancy in Pakistan. Thus the paragraphs that follow explore the level of religious and nonreligious (Pakistanis prefer the word "wordly" for this latter category) education of LeT militants that could be discerned from the biographies in our data set. A brief background on these different types of education in Pakistan precedes our analysis and is provided to contextualize our findings.

Nonreligious Education in Pakistan

<u>Background:</u> In the nonreligious educational sector—composed of public and private schooling—there are several levels of education: primary education (one to five years of schooling); secondary education, also called "middle" (six to eight years); and higher secondary (nine to ten years). [48] Upon completing ten years of education and successfully passing the relevant provincial textbook board exams, students are referred to as "matriculates" or "matrics." In Pakistan, students begin to specialize after the tenth grade. Should they continue into higher education, they will first achieve their FA or FSc, which typically takes an additional two years of schooling as well as sitting for an exam. These degrees are also referred to as higher secondary education certificates, intermediate certificates or sometimes "10+2." Students next can obtain a tertiary degree such as a BA or BS, which requires an additional two years of schooling. Upon completing a bachelor's degree, students may continue to do graduate degrees (e.g., MA, PhD). In addition, students may enter into professional programs (e.g., medicine, and engineering), which they can begin upon completion of their intermediate schooling (e.g., FA or FSc).[49]

Overall, nonreligious educational attainment in Pakistan is low. According to the Pakistan Social and Living Standards Measurement Survey, only 60 percent of Pakistanis have ever attended school (71 percent for males and 47 percent for females).[50]

---

[48] Even though Pakistan's public schools require the teaching of Islamic studies in their curriculum, we have decided to use the terms "nonreligious" or "secular" education for analytical clarity.

[49] C. Christine Fair, *The Madrassa Challenge: Militancy and Religious Education in Pakistan.* (Washington, D.C.: USIP, March 2008).

[50] See Pakistan Bureau of Statistics, "Pakistan Social and Living Standards Measurement Survey (2010–11)", table 2.1, http://www.pbs.gov.pk/sites/default/files/pslm/publications/pslm_prov2010-11/tables/2.1.pdf.

Only 49 percent of all Pakistanis have completed at least primary education (59 percent for males and 39 percent for females).[51] According to the most recent survey of 1998, which reports population by attainment levels (see Appendix C), slightly more than 17 percent of the population have attained the level of matriculation.

Results and Analysis: Most aspiring LeT fighters join the group when they are young, as the mean age of entry into the organization is a little over 16.9 years old. Figure 1, below, shows the distribution of education levels in our data, not counting those whose biographies did not provide this type of data.[52] The most common level of education completed is matric (tenth), with 44.3 percent of the militants entering LeT with this level of education. This finding is also consistent with our earlier report that the mean age of entry is 16.9, the age at which students would have just completed matric examinations. Only 17 percent of the militants have an educational level of intermediate or higher, while 22 percent stopped their education after "middle."

According to UNESCO statistics, in 2009 male enrollment in Pakistan's primary education was 86 percent, secondary education was 38 percent and tertiary education was 3 percent.[53] In our data, we see that 63 percent of LeT militants have at least a secondary education (matric or above), suggesting that their educational distribution is slightly higher than the national attainment levels, although the numbers are not exactly comparable.[54] This observation is consistent with Mariam Abou Zahab's finding that

recruits tend to be more educated than the average Pakistani and certainly more so than members of Deobandi jihadi groups, such as Sipah-e-Sahaba or Jaish-e-Mohammad. The majority of them have completed secondary school with high grades and quite a few have studied for BA [Bachelor of Arts] or BSc

---

[51] See Pakistan Bureau of Statistics, "Pakistan Social and Living Standards Measurement Survey," table 2.2, http://www.pbs.gov.pk/sites/default/files/pslm/publications/pslm_prov2010-11/tables/2.2.pdf.

[52] The biographies of 454 fighters provided this type of data (49 percent of our total observations).

[53] UNESCO Institute of Statistics, see http://stats.uis.unesco.org/unesco/TableViewer/document.aspx?ReportId=121&IF_Language=eng&BR_Co untry=5860&BR_Region=40535.

[54] In our data, we have educational attainment, while the UNESCO statistics are enrollment levels. Since one is a flow (enrollment) and the other a stock variable (attainment), they are not necessarily comparable to each other.

[Bachelor of Science] at college, and have come into contact with the LeT through da'wa programmes which have in turn led them to attend the big annual congregations organized every year in Muridke by the MDI [Markaz Dawa Al Irshad].[55]

A survey of militant families in Pakistan conducted by one of this paper's authors reached a similar conclusion.[56]

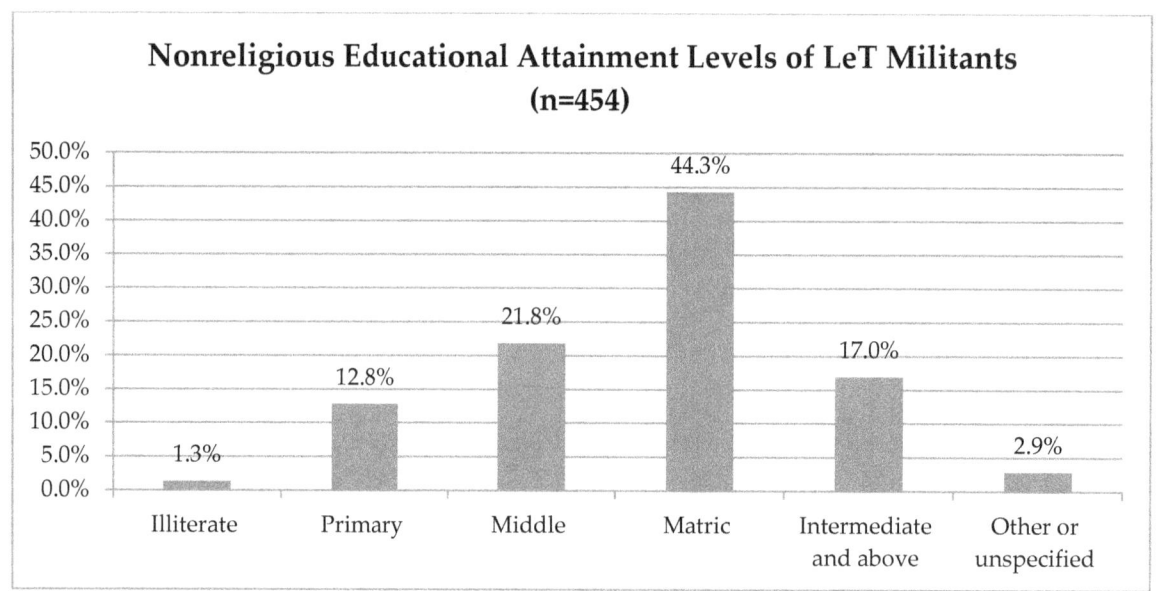

Figure 1: Nonreligious educational attainment levels of LeT recruits.

Religious Education in Pakistan

Background: There are several kinds of institutions and several means of acquiring a religious education in Pakistan. Parents may invite religious teachers to their homes. Pakistan's public schools require the teaching of Islamic studies in their curriculum. The educational market in Pakistan is constantly innovating, offering parents educational options that combine "worldly" with religious education.[57] Some madrassas (discussed below) are also teaching public school curriculum alongside their own regimented curriculum such that the students who graduate attain both religious credentials as well

---

[55] Abou Zahab, "I shall be waiting for you at the door of paradise," 137.
[56] C. Christine Fair, "The Educated Militants of Pakistan: Implications for Pakistan's Domestic Security," *Contemporary South Asia* 16:1 (March 2008), 100.
[57] Detailed in Fair, 2008.

as matriculation certificates.[58] Moreover, most of the children who do attend a madrassa attend one in combination with other schools. In this sense, madrassas typically complement other forms of education rather than serve as a substitute for the same.

Among those institutions that are dedicated solely to Islamic learning, the most basic is a mosque school (*maktab*). These institutions are ubiquitous in Pakistan. Students who obtain religious education at *maktab*s typically engage in basic studies such as how to read or properly recite the Qur'an (*nazira*). Some may undertake the challenge of memorizing the Qur'an (*Hifz-e-Qur'an*; one who has memorized the Qur'an is referred to as *hafez*). Another formal religious educational institution is the madrassa. (Unfortunately, many things are called madrassas that are not, e.g., militant training camps, militant housing, etc. Thus in this report we narrowly mean madrassa to be an actual place of regular Islamic learning.) Madrassas can be differentiated from *maktabs* in that only the former offer higher levels of Islamic learning that culminates in certificates of attainment (*sanad*). The sine qua non of a madrassa is that it teaches— either in full or in part—a specialized curriculum called *Dars-e-Nizami*, which boys usually complete in eight years at Sunni madrassas in Pakistan.[59] (For a schedule of religious degrees and their comparable attainment in the mainstream educational system in Pakistan, see Appendix D.)

Despite the sustained attention that madrassas in Pakistan garner from the policy community, few students overall exclusively attend a madrassa full-time. Pakistan's Federal Bureau of Statistics (FBS) routinely conducts national-level household economic surveys. These surveys query respondents regarding full-time enrollment of children in private, public and religious schools. Using such data from 1991 to 2001, Andrabi et al. estimate that madrassa enrollments account for less than 1 percent of children attending school full-time.[60] Because such household surveys may omit important populations (e.g., children in orphanages), Andrabi et al. adjusted their estimates upward to account for such exclusions. Even when assuming that all orphans in Pakistan attend a madrassa, they find that no more than 3 percent of children in school attend madrassas

---

[58] Ibid.

[59] "Girls complete a condensed curriculum in 6 years." See Fair. *The Madrassa Challenge.*

[60] Tahir Andrabi et al., "Religious School Enrollment in Pakistan: A Look at the Data" (working paper no. RWP05-024, John F. Kennedy School of Government, Harvard University, Cambridge, Massachusetts, March 2005).

full-time. This estimate comports well with the more recent survey-based findings of Cockcroft et al. That team, using information about madrassa enrollment obtained from a representative sample of 53,960 households, found that in 2004 a mere 2.6 percent of all children between 5 and 9 years of age attended a madrassa.[61]

Results and Analysis: Nearly 31 percent of biographies that were reviewed by the research team provided information about the level of religious education attained by LeT fighters. Based upon that data we find that 56.9 percent of LeT militants have attended a madrassa, with only 4.3 percent of those having received a *sanad*. Given the large amount of missing data for this variable, this finding suggests, but does not prove, that a higher percentage of LeT militants have spent time in a madrassa than prior studies have indicated. For example, in her pathbreaking study on LeT martyrs Mariam Abou Zahab noted that "the proportion of madrasa educated [LeT] boys is minimal (about 10 percent), but includes boys who studied in a madrassa after studying in an Urdu medium school."[62]

The number of years that militants attended these madrassas is an even more sparsely populated field, with only 5 percent of the data showing the number of years spent. Figure 2 below shows the distribution of the militants' level of religious educational attainment through a hierarchical chart. From the data, it is unclear whether a *hafez* actually referred to time spent in a madrassa or not, and so that link is dotted.

---

[61] Anne Cockcroft, et al., "Challenging the myths about madaris in Pakistan: A national household survey of enrolment and reasons for choosing religious schools," *International Journal of Educational Development* 29, no. 4 (July 2009), 342–349.

[62] Abou Zahab, "I shall be waiting for you at the door of paradise," 140. See also C. Christine Fair, "The Educated Militants of Pakistan: Implications for Pakistan's Domestic Security," *Contemporary South Asia* 16, no. 1 (March 2008), 100.

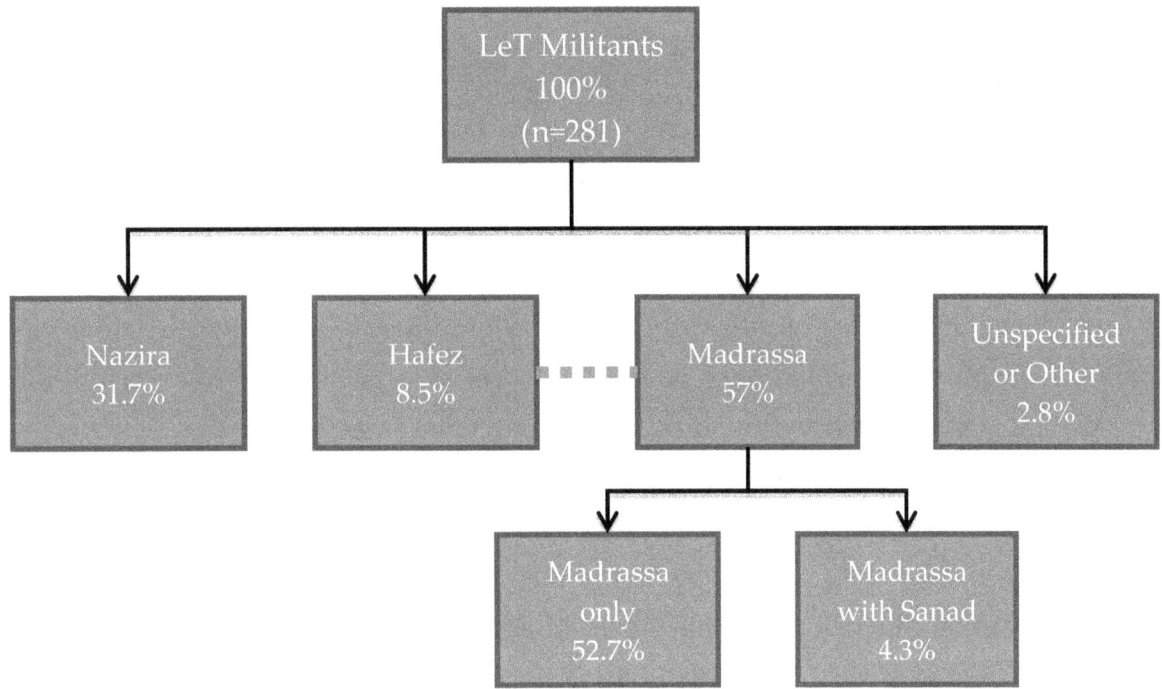

Figure 2: Militants' religious education (excluding missing data).

Based upon available data, militants spent an average of 2.77 years at a madrassa.[63] Recall from the above discussion that it takes three years on average to become a *hafez* and eight years to complete the *Dars-e-Nizami* curriculum. One explanation for what appears to be the relatively few number of years spent at a madrassa may be that unlike a regular madrassa student, who may attend not out of religious conviction but out of convenience or economic necessity, some of the men in our data set may have sought a religious education at an older age, suggesting that they may have been religiously inclined already. Our data shows that many militants did not attend a madrassa from the beginning of their education, but rather that many attended later.

The madrassas mentioned most frequently in our data set, many of which are known LeT-linked facilities in Pakistan's Punjab province, include LeT's main madrassa at its headquarters in Muridke, Ma'had al-Ala (twenty-nine times); Jamia Uloom e-Asria in Jhelum (four times); Jamia Muhammadia in Gujranwala (four times); and Jamia Muhammadia in Okara (three times), as well as several others.[64]

---

[63] This finding is identical with a survey of 141 militant families in Pakistan conducted by one of the authors. See Fair, "The Educated Militants of Pakistan," 101.

[64] According to Stephen Tankel, the enrollment at Ma'had al-Ala is estimated to be five hundred students. Tankel, *Storming the World Stage,* 70; four records labeled Markaz Taiba (a general reference to LeT's

Employment

Conventional wisdom on militancy in Pakistan and elsewhere states that militants tend to be less educated and are more likely to be poorer and underemployed or unemployed than their nonmilitant counterparts.[65] Investigating the prior occupations reveals three interesting findings.[66] First, LeT militants are typically low-income workers who come from the poor or middle-lower classes. The top five occupations of the militants, as revealed by the data, are factory worker, farmer, tailor, electrician and laborer. This finding corroborates Mariam Abou Zahab's observations: "Although the LeT claims that the mujahidin are recruited from all social classes, most of them belong to the lower middle class . . ."[67] Second, the number of LeT members on whom we have this type of data and who previously served in Pakistan's armed forces is remarkably small, only 7 out of 270, or less than 3 percent.[68] Third, only two people in our dataset of over nine hundred biographies were associated with a religious group as a previous form of employment.[69]

---

headquarters in Muridke) and six records for Jamia al-Dawa in Muridke (Jammat ud-Dawa's university located on that compound) are also found in our data set, although since they were not specifically described as Ma'had al-Ala madrassa they were excluded from the twenty-nine provided above. For background on Jamia Uloom-e-Asria, see http://jamia-asria.org/. Jamia Muhammadia Okara was founded in 1947 by Maulana Moinuddin Lakhvi—a relative of Zaki ur-Rehman Lakhvi. See "Ex-MNA Lakhvi Passes Away," *The News*, 10 December 2011. See also "Obituary: At Okara, the Patron of Markazi Jamiat Ahl-e-Hadees, former MNA Maulana Mueen-ud-Din Lakhvi expired," Radio Pakistan, 9 December 2011, www.radio.gov.pk/newsdetail-13736. According to one anonymous researcher interviewed for this report, Zaki ur-Rehman's mother is Moeenuddin Lakhvi's stepsister. Both Lakhvis are also believed to be from the same Lakhokay (village) caste. Two known LeT-linked madrassas in Karachi also show up in our data set twice: Jamia Abu Bakr and Jamaat-ul Dirasat ul-Islamiyah.

[65] See extensive discussion of these literatures in Graeme Blair et al., "Poverty and Support for Militant Politics: Evidence from Pakistan," *American Journal of Political Science* (available online 16 July 2012; forthcoming in print 2013).

[66] Only 29 percent of the biographies that were coded provided this type of data.

[67] Abou Zahab, "I shall be waiting for you at the door of paradise," 136.

[68] It is worth noting that our data only captures information about fighters who have died and not information about advisors, logisticians, trainers or (to our knowledge) senior level leaders. The data we have also represents the public story that LeT wants to communicate to the public, thus the group has an incentive to not report on its direct personnel linkages with the Pakistani military. In fact, such direct reporting might be a red line for the group. See the introduction for background on broader (public) linkages between LeT fighters and current and former Pakistani military members.

[69] One "gave the sermon at Jamia Masjid Dar ul Islam Khiyala" (*Majallahh al-Dawa*, March 1999) and the second served as "Imam of Jamia Masjid Quba in Shamsheer Town" (*Majallahh al-Dawa*, May 1999).

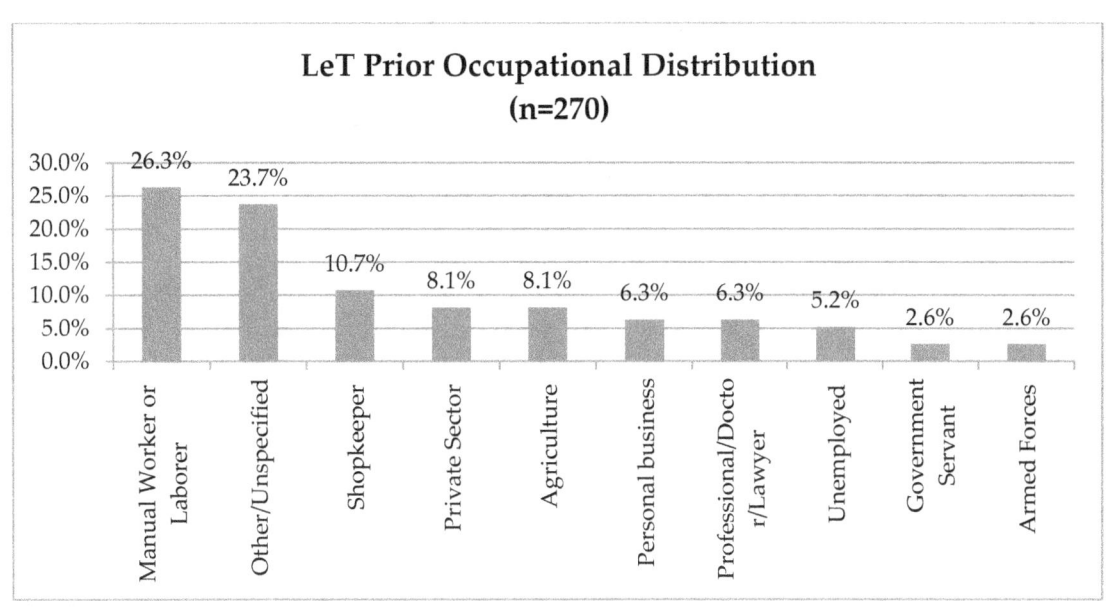

Figure 3: Prior Occupational Distribution.

In addition, to be able to compare the militants' occupations with the rest of the Pakistani population's, we coded the data according to the standard Federal Bureau of Statistics (FBS) occupational fields developed by the government of Pakistan.[70] The occupational distribution of men in Pakistan in 2001 through 2002, based upon this data, is represented in Figure 4 below.[71] The three main sectors in which men were employed in Pakistan over this time frame were factories (37 percent); sales, including shopkeepers (29 percent); and agriculture (13 percent). Ignoring the missing data, for those militants for whom we have information on prior occupations (a little more than 30 percent of the militants), we see that the most common FBS-aligned occupations are manual laborer or worker and shopkeeper.[72]

---

[70] Federal Bureau of Statistics of Pakistan. For background, see
http://web.archive.org/web/20110725144430/http://statpak.gov.pk/.

[71] The data is from FBS's household survey (HIES), a nationally representative survey. These statistics are reported in Zafar Mueen Nasir, "An Analysis of Occupational Choice in Pakistan: A Multinomial Approach," *Pakistan Development Review* 44,no. 1 (Spring 2005), 57–79.

[72] Most of the Unspecified or Other category was unspecified. Also included in this field are the occupations of driver, embroider, electrician, weaver and some other occupations that were not easy to classify in the existing categories.

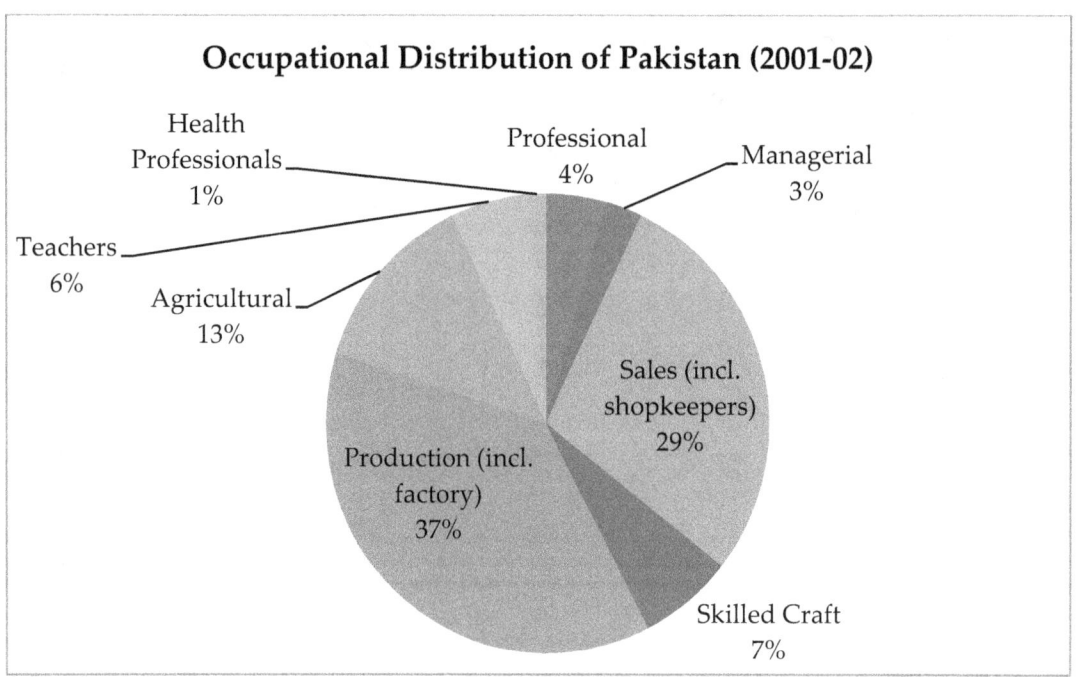

Figure 4: Occupational distribution of Pakistani men 2001 through 2002.

RESIDENCE AND RECRUITMENT

Scholars have long claimed that LeT is primarily a Punjabi organization and that its membership is mostly comprised of males from that Pakistani province.[73] In addition, scholars have also claimed that the Punjab has been fertile ground for Islamist militant groups other than the LeT since the late 1970s and early 1980s.[74] Leveraging our data, this section aims to move past these generalizations and to provide more granular insights into high-density areas of LeT recruitment and the specific recruitment methods employed by the organization in those locales.

Home Districts

Background: Pakistani administrative geography is structured into units inherited from British India. Pakistan is administratively divided into provinces, which are subdivided

---

[73] See, for example, Ashley Tellis, "The Menace that is Lashkar-e-Taiba," _Policy Outlook_ (Carnegie Endowment for International Peace, March 2012), 8, http://carnegieendowment.org/files/LeT_menace.pdf.
[74] For general background, see Arif Jamal, _A History of Islamist Militancy in Pakistani Punjab_, (Washington D.C.: Jamestown Foundation, 2011). For a snapshot of more recent dynamics, see "Fears Rise over Militants in Punjab," _Dawn_, undated, http://archives.dawn.com/archives/151763; "Jaish-e-Mohammed Builds Huge Base in Bahawalpur," _Daily Times_, 14 September 2009, www.dailytimes.com.pk/default.asp?page=2009%5C09%5C14%5Cstory_14-9-2009_pg7_16.

into divisions, which in turn are subdivided into districts. There are a total of 105 districts in Pakistan. (Pakistan has redistricted several times since independence.) Districts may be subdivided into *tehsils*, although some of the larger metropolitan areas or cities are their own districts.

Results and Analysis: From the martyr biographies, we know the location of the hometowns of the militants, as well as the districts and provinces in which they resided. This field is one of the most well-populated in our dataset, with nearly 70 percent of the 917 biographies' hometown districts being identified. We are thus able to provide detailed information on areas that produce large numbers of militants. As illustrated by Figure 5, our data confirms that most LeT militants are recruited from Pakistan's Punjab province. In our data, 89 percent of the militants are from Punjab, with 5 percent from Sindh, and about 3 percent from Khyber Pakhtunkhwa. A smaller number of militants originate from Azad Kashmir (about 0.5 percent), while Indian Kashmir, Gilgit-Baltistan and Baluchistan together produced about 1.1 percent of the militants in our sample. Three militants had hometowns in Afghanistan, two came from Saudi Arabia and one from Europe.[75]

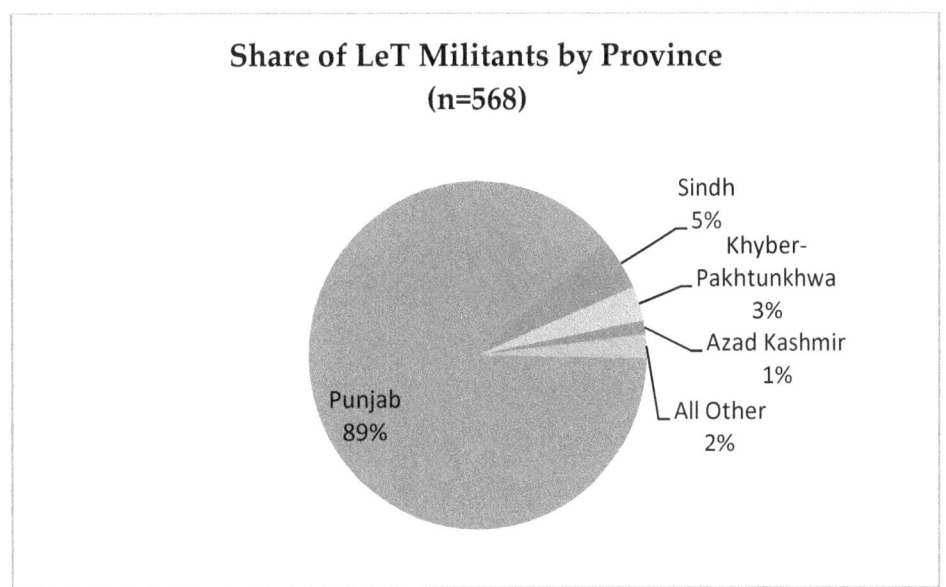

Figure 5: Share of LeT Militants by Province.[76]

---

[75] Both of the fighters from Afghanistan were from Nuristan province. One of the two LeT militants from Saudi Arabia was from Mecca. The other militant's hometown in Saudi Arabia was not disclosed. The country or hometown of the fighter from Europe was similarly not disclosed.

[76] The authors recognize that Azad Kashmir and Indian Kashmir are technically not provinces.

District-Level Details of Militant Origins

Figure 6 illustrates district-level details of recruitment of LeT militants. Each district is color coded by the number of militants originating from that district. As observed previously, the militants were recruited mostly from the Punjab region, but more interestingly, even within Punjab, greater numbers of militants seem to have originated from the areas that border India or are quite close to it.

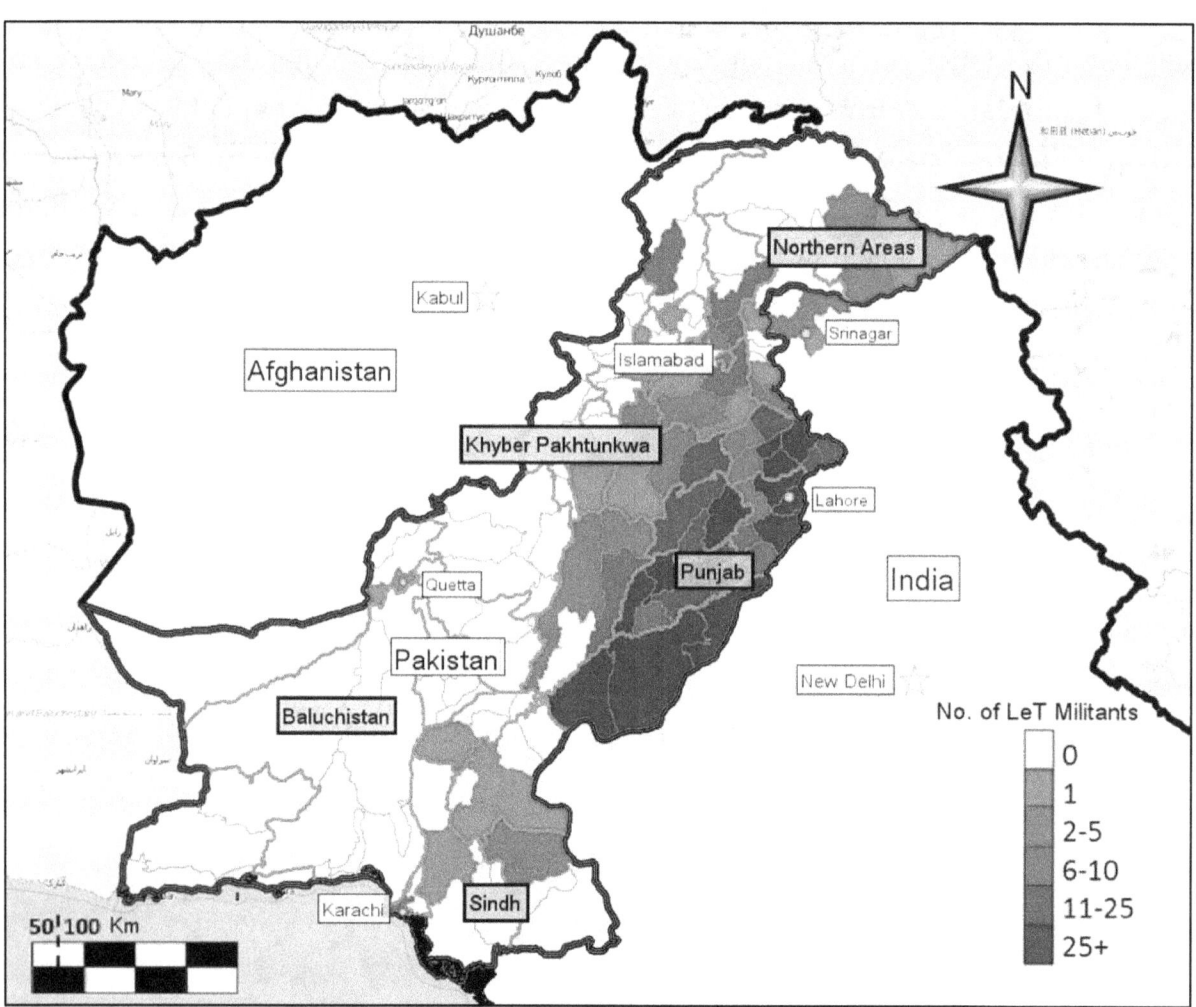

Figure 6: Distribution of LeT militants by district.

Table 1, below, shows the top ten districts by the number of militants that have originated from each district. As mentioned previously, the LeT militants in our study often came from densely populated and urbanized districts in the Punjab, with Gujranwala (10 percent), Faisalabad (10 percent) and Lahore (7 percent) producing more militants than any other district in the country.[77] This finding is not surprising, as those three areas have long been known to be locations where LeT is active and has a lot of infrastructure.[78]

District Name	Number of Militants	Percent Excluding Missing
Gujranwala	63	10 percent
Faisalabad	62	10 percent
Lahore	42	7 percent
Sheikhupura	35	5 percent
Kasur	34	5 percent
Sialkot	32	5 percent
Bahawalnagar	31	5 percent
Bahawalpur	31	5 percent
Khanewal	26	4 percent
Multan	26	4 percent
All Other Districts	258	40 percent
Missing Data	277	
Total	**917**	

Table 1: The top ten most LeT militant–producing districts in Pakistan.

[77] A similar analysis of the biographies of other Pakistani militant groups would likely yield rich details about differing recruitment patterns across groups. For example, an analysis of Jaish-e-Muhammad (JeM) fighters would likely reveal that a higher percentage of JeM militants are recruited from Bahawalpur than those from LeT, as Bahawalpur only accounts for 5 percent of LeT fighters in our data set. For background on JeM's presence in Bahawalpur, see Saeed Shah, "Terror Group Builds Big Base under Pakistani Officials' Noses," McClatchy, 13 September 2009, http://www.mcclatchydc.com/2009/09/13/75340/terror-group-builds-big-base-under.html.

[78] LeT's main complex in Muridke, Pakistan, is geographically located between two of these locations, being only 32 kilometers north from Lahore and 40 kilometers south from Gujranwala. For background on the Lahore connection, see Humeira Iqtidar, *Secularizing Islamists: Jama'at-e-Islami and Jamat'at-ud-Da'wa in Urban Pakistan* (Chicago: University of Chicago Press, 2011), 98–129; see also Yahya Mujahid's business card in U.S. Senate Foreign Relations Committee, "Lashkar-e-Taiba beyond Bin Laden: Enduring Challenges for the Region and the International Community," testimony prepared by Christine Fair, 24 May 2011, 19; for background on Faisalabad, see Marcela Gaviria, "Producers' Dispatches from the Field: Faisal Town," *PBS Frontline*, undated, www.pbs.org/wgbh/pages/frontline/shows/search/behind/23.html.

The concentration of militancy in certain districts is further revealed in Figure 7, where we display the cumulative percentage of LeT militants against the number of districts. Observe that 50 percent of all militants for which we have this type of data are recruited from the top ten districts, while nearly 80 percent of the militants come from the top twenty districts. Yet at the same time, our data also highlight that LeT recruitment is diversified across the north, central and southern Punjab districts, indicating that while there are specific districts in which we see a high concentration of fighters, LeT recruitment is not a geographically isolated phenomenon within that particular province. Future studies into the recruitment practices of other Punjabi-based militant groups with infrastructural hubs located in specific Punjab districts, such as Jaish-e-Muhammad and its base in the southern district of Bahawalpur, could reveal interesting findings about potential overlapping districts of recruitment and the nature of how militant groups compete for local recruits in those areas.

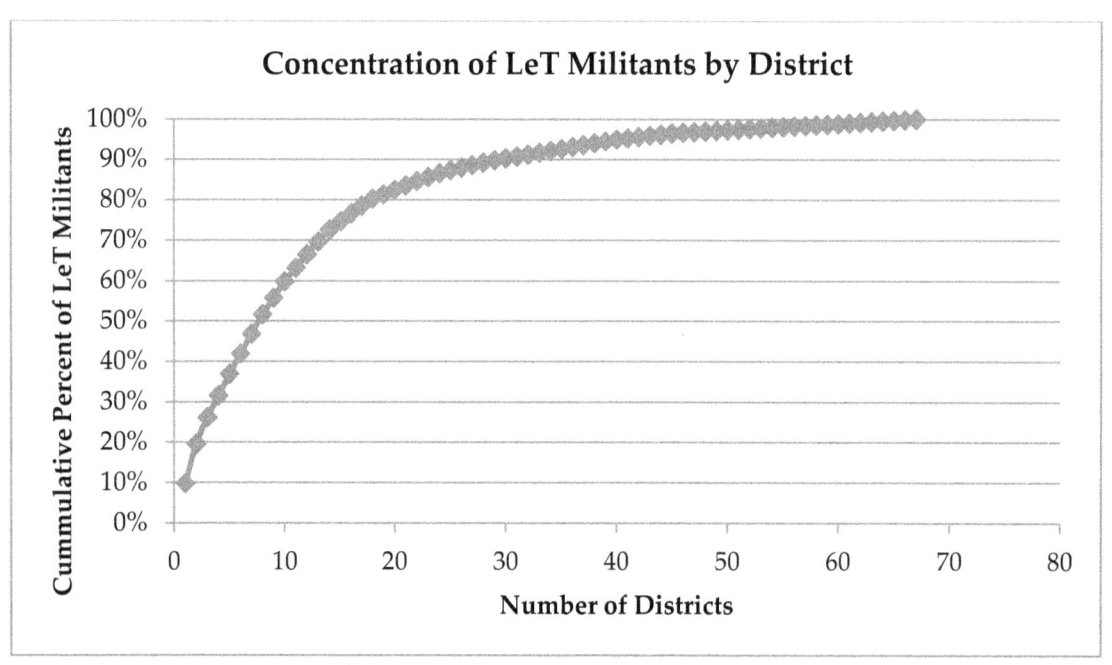

Figure 7: Cummulative percentage of LeT militants by the number of districts.

Means of Recruitment

Background: As with all militant groups, recruitment is one of the primary activities needed to sustain LeT. Given the broad range of activities in which the group is engaged, LeT trains far more people than it will ever deploy on any mission. The majority of persons recruited by the organization are therefore likely expected to return to their localities and proselytize on behalf of LeT and its interpretation of the Ahl-e-Hadith school of Islamic jurisprudence. This is consistent with LeT's belief that one must also extend the invitation to others (da`wa) to reform Pakistani society from within by purporting its worldview or to engage in jihad.[79]

Results and Analysis: There is no one single or centralized method through which LeT members are recruited, but instead, as one would expect, the group uses a slew of methods.[80] Based upon our data, we were able to identify and code twelve different channels of LeT recruitment.[81] We have information on the means of recruitment for 362 observations, which is 39 percent of our data. We find that militants are rarely recruited through more than one channel,[82] as over 90 percent of our militant recruitment data identify only a single channel. The biographies of 8 percent of the individuals indentify two channels of recruitment, while fewer than 2 percent of the militants were recruited by three separate channels.

Figure 8, below, shows the distribution associated with our twelve LeT recruitment channels. The most common form of recruitment is by a current member of LeT, as noted in 20 percent of the cases.[83] The second-most-common form of recruitment is when a family member, almost always a brother or the father, helps an individual to join the group (20 percent of all cases).[84] LeT propaganda, which includes speech or

---

[79] C. Christine Fair, "Lashkar-e-Tayiba and the Pakistani State" *Survival* 53, no. 4 (August-September 2011), 29-52.

[80] For example, recruiters wait to enlist young men at schools, on the street and outside buildings. For example, see *Majallah al-Dawa*, July 2001, 52; LeT recruiters also pass out magazines, literature and pamphlets in select areas. See *Majallah al-Dawa*, March 1997, 35–40; *Majallah al-Dawa*, July 1997, 44–45.

[81] These channels include recruitment by a family member, a friend, an LeT member, the LeT student wing or a general acquaintance and at a mosque, a madrassa or an LeT conference. It also includes those who self-initiated, who joined the group after being exposed to LeT's propaganda or those who joined via other means or after having been a member of Hizbul Mujahidin (a militant group that has historically been active in Indian Kashmir).

[82] Although it is possible that the most important channel is not listed in the biography, or that other channels are selectively listed.

[83] For background on the concept of da`wa, see "Understanding Islamism," *International Crisis Group Middle East/North Africa Report*, no. 37 (2 March 2005), www.crisisgroup.org/en/regions/middle-east-north-africa/north-africa/037-understanding-islamism.aspx.

[84] For a breakdown of those included in the term "family," see Appendix A.

literature,[85] is the channel for the recruitment of 12 percent of militants, which when added to those who are self-initiated (4 percent), can be considered the share of militants who are recruited passively by LeT. Mosques (9 percent) and madrassas and Islamic study centers (8 percent) together account for 17 percent of recruitment. Interestingly, there is evidence of limited overlap between LeT and Hizbul Mujahidin (another militant group historically focused on Indian Kashmir) members, as fewer than 3 percent of individuals are recruited into LeT by that other militant group. Three percent of individuals also mention an LeT conference, such as the group's annual convention (*ijtima*), or another similar conference as the channel through which they were recruited.[86]

These findings are considerably different from those derived from a previous study of 141 militant households (associated with a mix of militant groups, not just LeT) in Pakistan.[87] That results from that study suggested that religious gatherings, family and friends played a much stronger role in the recruitment of that sample of militants than was the case for the fighters from our data set, highlights—as one might assume—that there is likely variation in the recruitment methods across groups in Pakistan.

---

[85] If an individual is said to have decided to join LeT as a result of hearing a particular speech or reading particular jihadi material, we classified the individual as being influenced by propaganda as a means of recruitment.

[86] For examples, see the biographies of Abu Usman Farooq Ahmed (*Majallah al-Dawa*, October 2001, 42–43) and Abu Muawwiyah Muhammad Asif (*Majallah al-Dawa*, April 2000, 37–38).

[87] Only 13 of the 141 militant families interviewed (9 percent) were affiliated with LeT. For details, see C. Christine Fair, "The Educated Militants of Pakistan: Implications for Pakistan's Domestic Security," *Contemporary South Asia* 16, no. 1 (March 2008), 99–100.

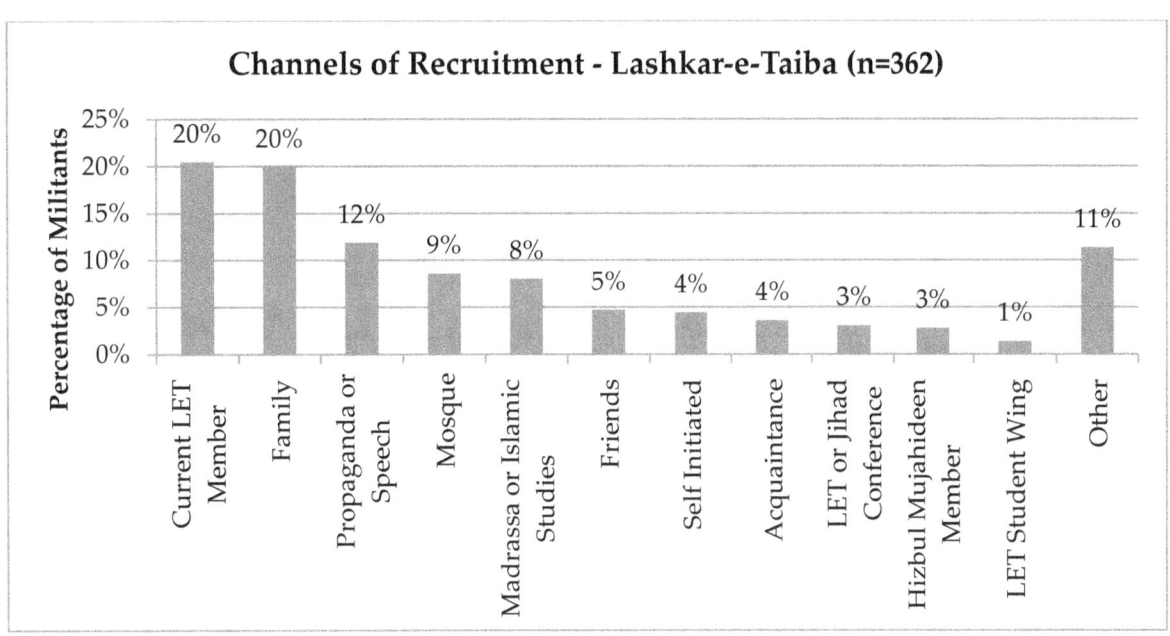

Figure 8: LeT channels of recruitment.

Recruitment Channel Variation over Time

To understand how recruitment channels may have become more or less popular over time, we ploted the channels of recruitment over the year of publication of the martyr biography, which we used as our time dimension. We restricted our sample to the years 1997 to 2004, when we have at least twenty nonmissing observations for the recruitment channel variable.[88]

Figure 9, below, shows the top three channels over time. The graph reveals an interesting finding: the recruitment through current LeT members seemed to have peaked around 2000 and 2001, when nearly 30 percent of the recruitment was made through this channel. There is also a strong upward trend in recruitment through family members, typically fathers and brothers. Since 2000, every year the share of recruitment through this channel has increased over the previous year, and by 2004, this channel contributed to over 40 percent of LeT recruitment. Recruitment as a result of propaganda or speech has been relatively stable over the sample period.

---

[88] Our overall time period is from 1994 through 2007, but there are very few nonmissing observations in these outlying years for percentage comparisons to be meaningful.

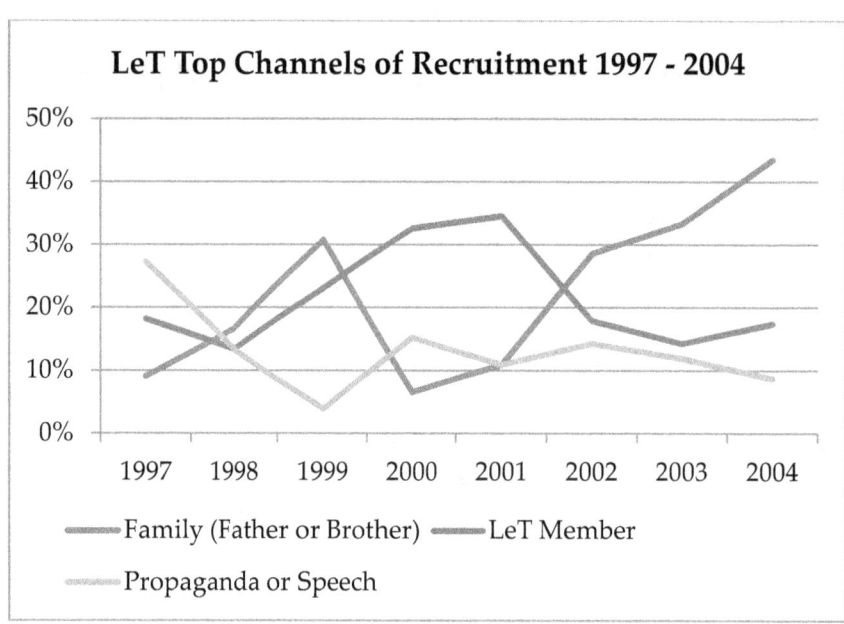

Figure 9: Top three channels of LeT recruitment over time.

The fourth- and fifth-largest channels of recruitment, mosques and madrassas, also display an interesting trend. Figure 10, below, plots these two channels across the same time period. Observe that there is a steady negative trend on the importance of mosques in this time period, and in 2004 their contribution was zero. Madrassas' contribution is relatively more stable, at about 10 percent, but neither of these two channels seems to be increasing in relative importance as a means of recruitment. Without additional data it is not possible to identify whether these trends are driven by selection issues, a change in how LeT reports or describes recruitment in their magazines or if they actually reflect a shift in LeT recruitment.

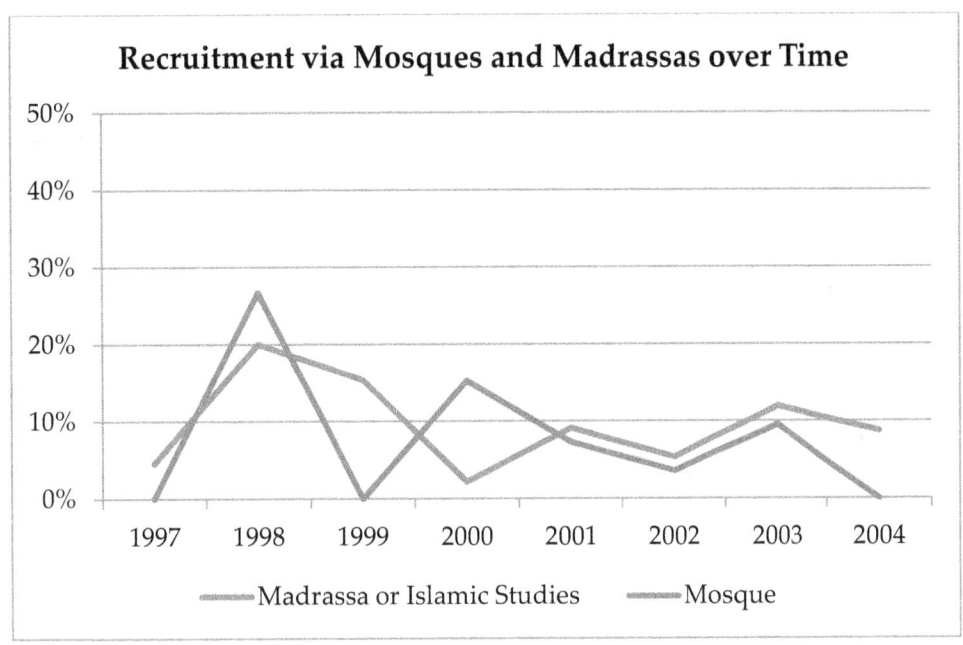

Figure 10: LeT Recruitment from mosques and madrassas over time.

TRAINING AND DEPLOYMENT

The scale and scope of LeT's training is extensive. While not all who receive training see combat in places like Indian Kashmir, some estimates suggest that between 100,000 to 300,000 men have received some form of LeT training over the last two decades.[89] This estimate also includes a smaller number of Western jihadists who, after receiving training from LeT, have played active roles in a number of international terrorism plots.[90] The continuation, reach and legacy of LeT's training programs have emerged as a central concern for counterterrorism practitioners as a result. To that end, this section investigates the training, deployment and death of LeT militants. Specific attention is placed on examining the type, length and location of LeT training; the location of death of LeT militants at country and district levels; and how the latter has changed over time.

---

[89] "According to reliable sources, between 100,000 and 300,000 young men underwent [LeT] military training." See Mariam Abou Zahab and Olivier Roy, *Islamist Networks: The Afghan-Pakistan Connection*, (London: Hurst 2002), 39.

[90] See, for example, the discussion of the case of David Headley, LeT's lead reconnaissance operative for the November 2008 Mumbai attacks in Sebastian Rotella, "A Perfect Terrorist", Pro Publica, transcript, undated, www.pbs.org/wgbh/pages/frontline/afghanistan-pakistan/david-headley/transcript-13/; see also the case of Willie Brigitte (for a summary see, Regina v Lodhi [2006] NSWSC, 638).

Training: Type, Length and Location

Background: In addition to a number of specialized courses, LeT has three primary types of training, the first two of which are progressive. They include:

Daura-e-Aama (Basic Training) is LeT's basic three-week training course. During this twenty-one-day course, attendees are given religious instruction (i.e., learn parts of the Qur'an and how to perform Islamic rituals in the Ahl-e-Hadith way), training in light arms, particularly in the use of the Kalashnikov and hand grenades, and instruction in basic guerilla warfare tactics.

Daura-e-Khasa (Specialized Training) is LeT's advanced training course, which lasts for three months.[91] This program is usually reserved for those trainees who are likely to be sent to Indian-administered Kashmir (or even to other parts of India) or to other places to wage armed jihad. This advanced course is "geared towards guerilla warfare, with training in the use of arms and ammunition, ambush and survival techniques."[92]

Other Named Training includes a number of LeT training courses about which not much is known. These courses are believed to be both physical and ideological in orientation (see below for more information) and to either occur after *Daura-e-Khasa* or as modules to complement that same course.

Results and Analysis: Out of a pool of 627 militants whose biographies provided this type of data, 5 percent of the militants were said to have undergone only basic training (*Daura-e-Aama*). The highest level of training reported by most of the LeT militants (62 percent) was specialized training (*Daura-e-Khasa*), and an additional 12 percent were able to name other specific training courses, which potentially followed *Daura-e-Aama* ("Specialized Named or Other Named" in Figure 11 below). Since the majority of these trainings are named after companions of the Prophet Muhammad and other historically important figures in Islamic history, it is possible that in addition to having physical elements to them, many of these courses were also ideological or religious in

---

[91] Arif Jamal interview with Abu Ahad, March 2006, Muzaffarabad.

[92] B. Raman, "The Lashkar-e-Taiba (LeT)," South Asia Analysis Group Paper 374, 15 December, 2001, www.southasiaanalysis.org/papers4/paper374.html; Muhammad Amir Rana, *The A to Z of Jehadi Organizations in Pakistan* (Lahore: Mashall Books, 2004), 58.

orientation. Examples of these other "named" trainings in the data are *Daura-e-Saqeela*, *Daura-e-Abdullah bin Masood*, or *Daura-e-Ribat*, the latter of which provides instruction in intelligence collection.[93] (For a full list of these named trainings and the frequencies with which they appear in the biographies, see the Data Appendix that accompanies this report.)

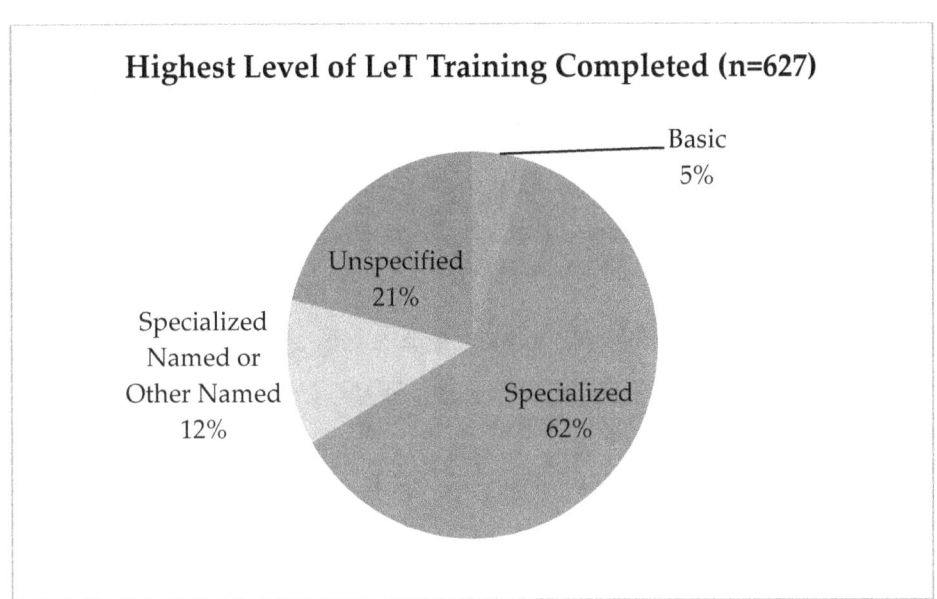

Figure 11: Type of LeT Training.

Training Length, and Time Spent Between Basic Training and Death

As mentioned above, the length of training varies across the different types of training LeT provides, ranging anywhere from three weeks to ten months. Figure 12, below, shows the mean lengths of different LeT training types.

---

[93] Source for *Daura-e-Ribat*: see Stephen Tankel, *Storming the World Stage,* 78, 90 and note 328.

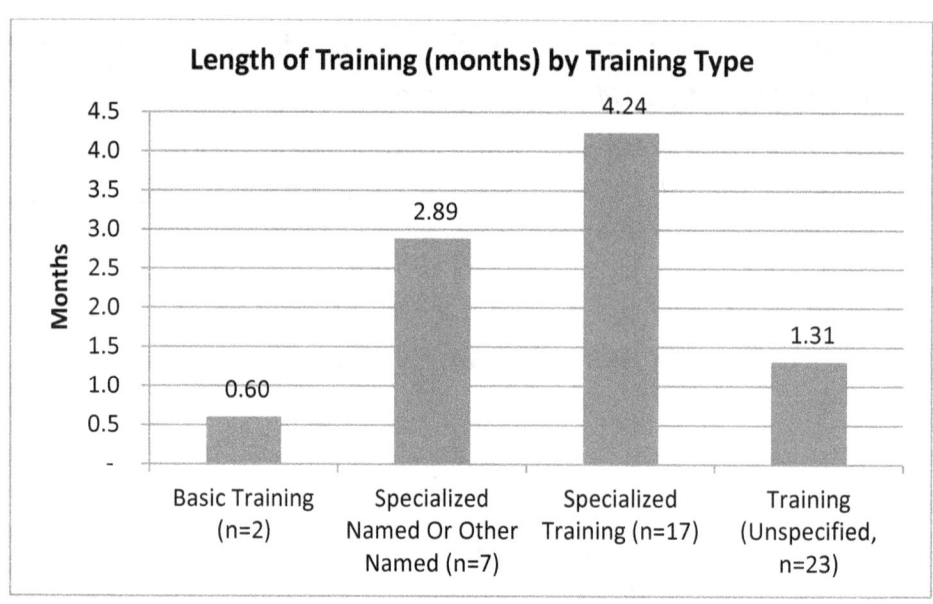

Figure 12: Mean length of each type of training.

A review of the biographies suggests that after completing basic training the trainees usually spend the next few years waiting to be deployed. This is consistent with our data, as only 5 percent of the militants studied died within one year of their entry into the organization, with the median amount of time a militant spent between joining the organization and death being 4.0 years.[94] The time in between the militants' initial recruitment and deployment is spent completing basic and specialized training, completing service (*khidmat*) at an LeT camp, proselytizing (*da`wa*) on behalf of the group, continuing with their jobs and sometimes even doing nothing.[95] In cases where

---

[94] We are measuring entry into LeT as being either the time at which a recruit joined the group or went for basic training.

[95] *Majallah al-Dawa*, April 2001, 44. For example, certain individuals in our data set worked at an LeT hospital, as a writer or in LeT's communications department before being deployed. See the biographies of Abu Ammar Muhammad Naeem Sajid (*Mothers* 2,, 107–111), Abu Hanzala Dawud ul-Hasan (*Majallah al-Dawa*, December 2000, 43–44), Abu Sayyaf Babar Waheed (*Mothers* 3, 208–211), and Dr. Abu Musab Sanaullah (*Majallah al-Dawa*, November 2001, 46–47). This finding also corroborates Mariam Abou Zahab's analysis on basic training: "First they attend an ordinary course (*daura-e amma*) that lasts 21 days and focuses on religious education and more precisely on the principles of the Ahl-e Hadith school of thought; two weeks are devoted to religious education and one week to practical *da'wa* and *tabligh*. They are then sent back home to resume their former activities, and to engage in *da'wa* work in their neighborhood, with the particular task of recruiting their friends. They remain under the scrutiny of the local LeT leaders who only agree to send them for the three-month special course (*daura-e khassa*) after assessing their level of motivation." Mariam Abou Zahab, "Salafism in Pakistan: The Ahl-e Hadith Movement," *Global Salafism: Islam's New Religious Movement*, Roel Meijer, ed. (New York: Columbia University Press, 2009), 126–142.

LeT orders young men to serve, it is possible that the effort is to keep the organization running functionally but also to keep the young men connected to the organization while they mature. Such an approach could also be a way for LeT to manage its image with the local community, as the recruitment and deployment of youth who are too young appears to be an issue that some resent.[96]

Training Locations

A total of 154 LeT fighter biographies (less than 20 percent of all observations) provided information about where those militants received trained. As Figure 13 shows, LeT training has historically occurred in Muzaffarabad, Pakistan, (47 percent) and in Afghanistan (28 percent).[97] Together these two locations accounted for 75 percent of all LeT militant training in our dataset.

---

[96] According to the testimonials, while the militants wait for permission to be deployed, they frequently petition senior members of LeT, such as Hafez Saeed and Zaki ur-Rehman Lakhvi, to grant them approval. LeT leaders are reported to often express hesitancy in letting younger militants fight because the militants are too young or are not ready. During this dwell time LeT leaders usually delay their deployment by having them do some other work. For example, one of the biographies noted that "he wanted to go for specialized training, but Hafez Sahib [likely a reference to Hafiz Saeed] put him on duty in Peshawar for three months." Eventually, the leaders provide approval for the youth to fight, but the logic that compels them to deploy the young men is not always discussed in the biographies studied as part of this report. In some cases, the stated logic may be as simple as the militant's being able to grow a beard, a marker of age and religiosity to LeT. For example, see *Majallah al-Dawa*, July 1999, 43.

[97] LeT is believed to have had at least two training camps in Afghanistan. One camp was known as Muaskar-e-Taiba in Paktia province, and the second, Muaskar-e-Aqsa, was located in Kunar province. See Yoginder Sikand, "The Islamist Militancy in Kashmir: The Case of the Lashkar-e-Taiba," in *The Practice of War: Production, Reproduction and Communication of Armed Violence*, Aparna Rao et al., eds, (New York: Berghahn Books, 2007), 215–238; Mariam Abou Zahab, "I Shall be Waiting at the Door of Paradise," 133–158; Saeed Shafqat, "From Official Islam to Islamism: The Rise of Dawat-ul-Irshad and Lashkar-e-Taiba," in Christophe Jaffrelot, ed., *Pakistan: Nationalism without a Nation* (London: Zed Books, 2002), 131–147. Note that Kunar is known to be home to numerous Ahl-e-Hadith adherents in Afghanistan, which overall has few followers in that country. For this reason, Kunar has been an attractive safe haven in Afghanistan for Arab and other foreign fighters who follow a similar ideological orientation.

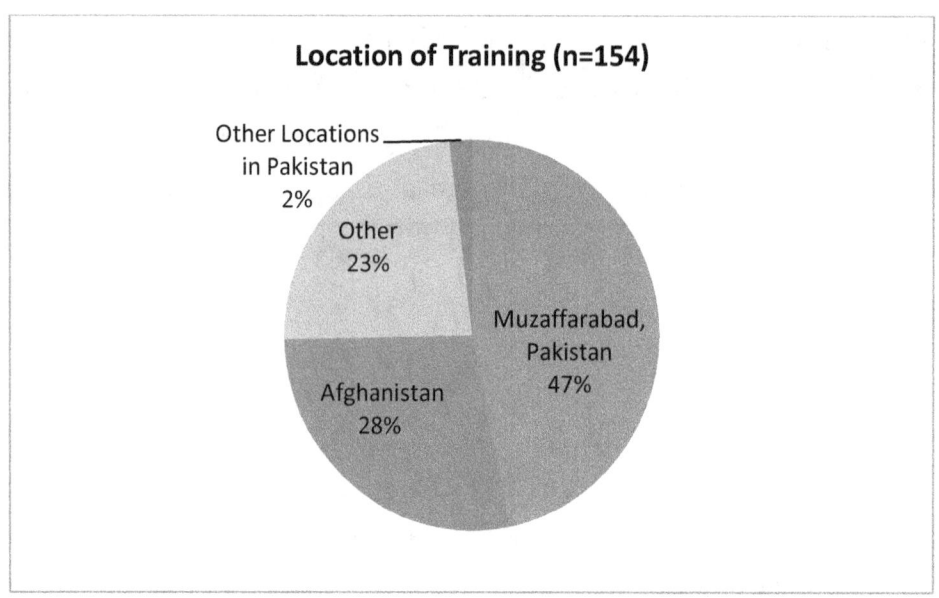

Figure 13: Location of LeT fighter training.

The locations' order of prevelance (as displayed above) does not change when only those LeT members who received specialized training are considered.[98] As we see in Figure 14 below, Muzaffarabad's share gets slightly larger and Muaskar-e-Taiba in Afghanistan's share gets slightly lower in such case.

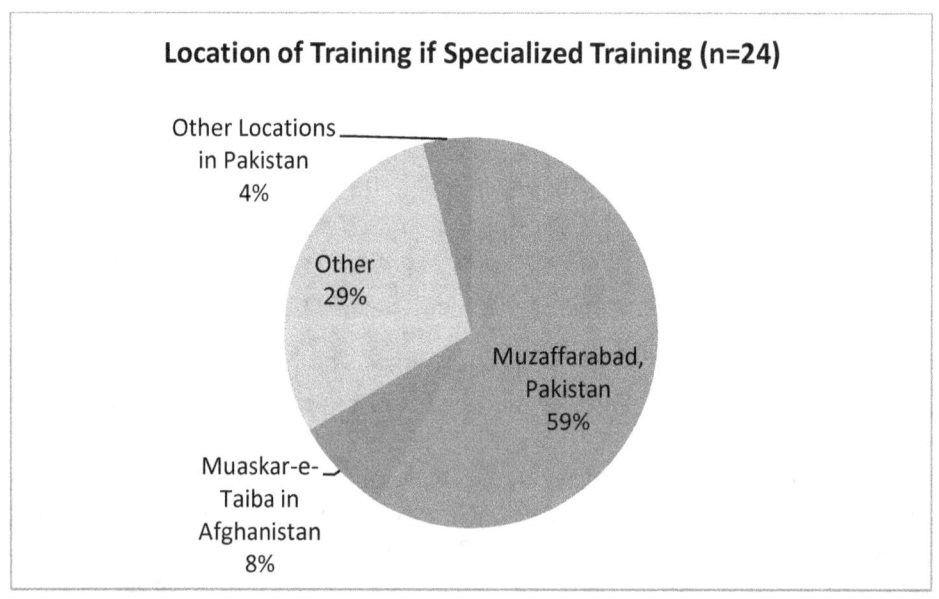

Figure 14: Location of training for those LeT members who received specialized training.

---

[98] For the purposes of this graphic "specialized" includes both "specialized" and "specialized named or other named trainings." For background see Appendix A.

Fighting Fronts and Location of Death

Results and Analysis: LeT's primary fighting front has historically been Indian Kashmir. Of the individuals for whom we have data in this field, 779 out of 822 list Indian Kashmir as a fighting front, representing 94 percent of the individuals.[99] Thirty nine individuals identify Afghanistan as a fighting front. Even among these militants (who make up 5 percent of the overall data set), 32 of these 39 also list Indian Kashmir as a fighting front. Two individuals appear to have fought in at least three conflict zones: Afghanistan, Tajikistan and Chechnya (one of these fighters also lists a fourth – Bosnia – as a fighting front).[100]

From the martyr biographies, we also have details on the location of death. Table 2 shows the country of death for the militants. Not surprisingly, over 94 percent of the militants died in India, mostly in Indian Kashmir, which is consistent with our finding that the most active fighting front for LeT militants is Indian Kashmir.

Location of Death—Country	No. LeT Militants	Percent	Percent, Excluding Missing
Afghanistan	5	0.5%	0.7%
India	660	72.2%	94.4%
Pakistan	19	2.1%	2.7%
Line of Control	13	1.4%	1.9%
Missing	215	23.5%	
Total	912		

Table 2: Location of death (country-level) for LeT militants.

[99] The state of Jammu and Kashmir is divided into three regions, Jammu, Kashmir and Ladakh. Each of these regions are subdivided into districts. Jammu and Kashmir regions are each divided into ten districts, while the Ladakh region, which is smaller in comparison, comprises two districts.

[100] Both of these individuals appear to be foreign fighters and unfortunately, even though their biographies were published in LeT magazines, their association with the group is not entirely clear. Given the information provided, the individuals identified by LeT as Abu Khatib and Abu Waleed (who went to four fighting fronts) are likely the relatively high-profile commanders Samer Bin Saleh Bin Abdullah Al-Swelim and Abd Al-Aziz Bin Ali Bin Said Al Said Al-Ghamdi (respectively). For general background on each, see M. B. Nokhcho and Glen. E. Howard, "Chechnya's Abu Walid and the Saudi Dilemma," *Terrorism Monitor* 2, no. 1 (15 January 2004), www.jamestown.org/single/?no_cache=1&tx_ttnews%5Btt_news%5D=26227; for biographical data provided by LeT see *Mahanah Zarb-e-Taiba*, November 2004, 30–33 and *Mahanah Zarb-e-Taiba*, October 2004, 35–38. These two fighters could have been highlighted in LeT's magazine due to their prestige, because of potential personal relationships that they forged with LeT cadre in Afghanistan or because the editor or writer might have just been looking to fill space in those particular magazine editions.

At the district level, we have details on the location of death for 465 militants, which is 51 percent of all the biographies in our data. Table 3 below displays the top ten districts in which militants were killed. Together these districts are the location of 93 percent of all militant deaths, and the top three districts—Kupwara, Baramulla, and Poonch, all in Indian Kashmir—account for almost half of all militants killed.[101]

Location of Death— District	Number of Militants	Share of Militants (excl. missing)	Cumulative Percent
Kupwara	128	27.5 percent	27.5 percent
Baramulla	52	11.2 percent	38.7 percent
Poonch	47	10.1 percent	48.8 percent
Budgam	46	9.9 percent	58.7 percent
Rajouri	34	7.3 percent	66.0 percent
Bandipore	27	5.8 percent	71.8 percent
Doda	26	5.6 percent	77.4 percent
Anantnag	25	5.4 percent	82.8 percent
Srinagar	24	5.2 percent	88.0 percent
Udhampur	21	4.5 percent	92.5 percent

Table 3: Top ten districts for the location of death for LeT Militants.

Changes in Location of LeT Deaths between 1990 and 2004

In addition to the location of death of the militants in our study, we also know the year of their death. While it is not clear how representative our data set is of all LeT fighter deaths, this data can still be leveraged to form impressions about areas in Indian Kashmir where militant activity is potentially growing or decreasing. In our analysis, we divide the year of death into three five-year groups: 1990 to 1994, 1995 to 1999 and 2000 to 2004.[102] We created these categories to ensure a minimum number of militants in

---

[101] Our district-level findings are in line with anecdotal information about LeT's historical areas of presence in Indian Kashmir. For example, see information about Kupwara, Budgam, Doda, Rajouri and Poonch in K. Santhanam Sreedhar and Sudhir Saxena Manish, *Jihadis in Jammu and Kashmir: A Portrait Gallery* (New Delhi: SAGE Publications 2003).

[102] There are only four observations that fall outside of these year grouping categories, three in 1989 and one in 2008.

each group, and also so that any trends identified can be considered over a longer length of time as opposed to being perhaps the result of random yearly shocks.

Figure 15 below summarizes the findings. In Figure 15, we separated out the top five districts where LeT militants have died, which are Kupwara, Baramulla, Poonch, Budgam and Rajouri, and also created a category for "all other districts."[103] The numbers in the graph are the actual number of militants that were killed in each district in that year group. The share of each district can be read from the vertical axis.

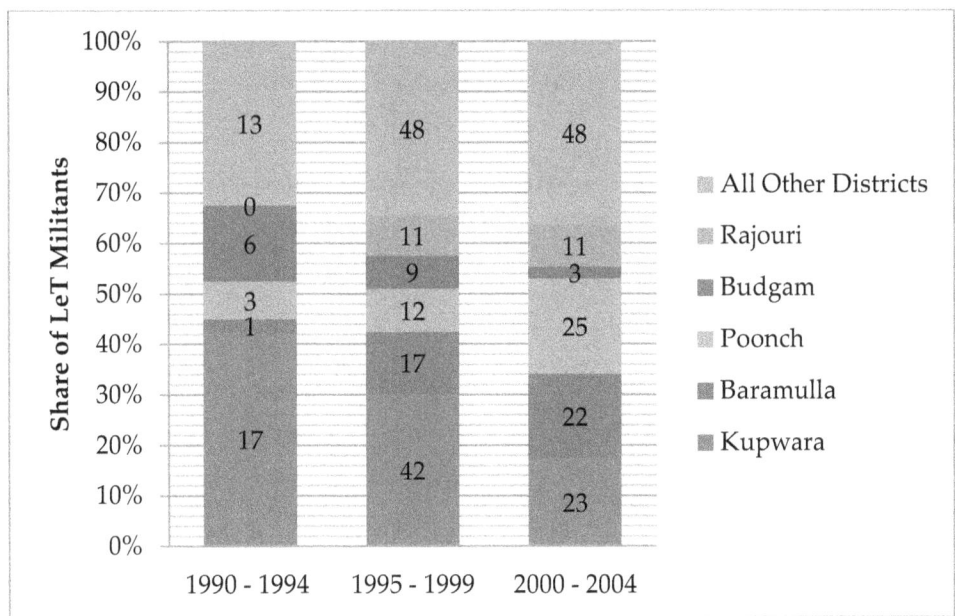

Figure 15: The location of death of LeT militants over time.

This figure lends itself to a number of interesting observations. First, observe that around 70 percent of LeT militants are killed consistently in the top five districts across all years. However, there is considerable heterogeneity between these districts.

Kupwara, the district with the largest number of militants killed, appears to be becoming less important overall as a fighting area, with its share of deaths declining during each year group. Baramulla and Poonch both of which had relatively low number of militants killed in the early 1990s, have been increasing in both their number

---

[103] Unless specifically stated, the authors made the assumption that references to Poonch district (it being a district that exists in both India-administered Kashmir and Pakistan-administered Kashmir) were to the Poonch district on the Indian side of the Line of Control.

and their share of LeT deaths over time. While throughout the 1990s, Kupwara was far and away the district with the largest number of militant deaths, by the first half of the decade of the 2000s, Poonch, Baramulla and Kupwara were together and jointly the largest locations of LeT deaths.

Among the districts that rank fourth and fifth in terms of the number of fighters killed in a particular location, Budgam district's share of militants killed has been decreasing, while Rajouri district, which did not have much militant death activity in the early 1990s, is now the fourth-largest location of militant deaths for LeT. These trends indicate that the areas of LeT fighter deaths in Indian Kashmir have become more geographically distributed over time, suggesting that the group has intentionally pursued this type of strategy or that it is potentially in response to pressure applied — or new campaigns waged — by Indian security services in select districts.[104]

Conclusion

Our data attest to the enduring nature of LeT and its sustained ability to attract high-quality recruits from across the Punjab and through a variety of means for operations throughout South Asia. This research contributes to the evolving body of literature that suggests that poverty, limited education and time spent at a madrassa are poor predictors for determining either support for terrorism or participation in terrorism in Pakistan. If our data are at all representative of LeT's other cadres, they would appear to suggest that some of Pakistan's best-educated young men are being dispatched to die in this unending conflict with India. While every opportunity to improve CVE programming in Pakistan should be pursued, our data also suggest that CVE programming cannot diminish the ability of LeT to recruit, retain and deploy militants in the service of the organization unless such programs can understand the appeal that LeT and other militant organizations offer to young fighters and their families in Pakistan. For CVE programming in Pakistan to be effective, it would have to undermine the trust that exists between LeT and members of Pakistani society, and counter the narrative that LeT is an instrument for positive change. This will likely prove to be a

---

[104] Other variables, such as local political factors or responses taken by local communities in those areas, could have also contributed to this dynamic.

significant challenge, given the range of LeT's social service activities, and one that will require further study and a significant investment in time and resources.

APPENDIX A: DATA CODING AND CATEGORIES

This appendix summarizes the data coding and categories that were created from the LeT biographies reviewed for this report.

General

- *Year of Publication:* The year of the publication associated with a particular biography.

Fighter Background

- *Name/Alias:* The name or alias the militant adopted or that was assigned by the organization.

- *Marriage status:* This field was only coded "yes" or "no" if the biography explicitly provided information about a fighter's marital status. If the biography mentioned that the fighter had been married, but had since been divorced, this was coded as "yes (divorced)." If a biography did not provide this type of information, it was coded as "N/A."

- *Children:* The number of children the militant had.

- *Brothers:* The number of brothers the militant had.

- *Sisters:* The number of sisters the militant had.

- *Religious education:* The highest level of religious education that was identified in the biographies. This ranged from an ability to read/recite the Qur'an to significant education at a madrassa. Five possible categories—*nazira*, *hafez*, madrassa, *sanad* and unspecified/other—were coded in this field. These categories are imperfect. However, we sought to maximize information from the biographies, which forced us to minimize the numbers of categories into which we could extract information. The first category we coded was *nazira*, which was coded positively if the militant read or recited the Qur'an. The second category was *hafez*. We coded this in the affirmative if the militant completed the memorization of the Qur'an (*Hifz-e-Qur'an*). If the militant memorized (*hifz*) half or a portion the Qur'an, the militant's level of religious attainment would be classified as *nazira*, and not *hafez*. (Note that this is a coding rule, not a description of the schedule of Islamic learning.) As noted in the section on religious education, it typically takes three years for a student to memorize the Qur'an, but it can take longer for students with less aptitude, and it can take less time for those who are more talented. The third category is madrassa. We coded this in the affirmative if a militant's biography indicated that he attended a madrassa but did not obtain a degree or achieve *nazira* or *hafez* status. This is because many students attend a madrassa but do not complete enough of the program to achieve even the lowest *sanad* (a certificate). The fourth category, *sanad,* was coded in the affirmative only if the militant obtained a certificate at a religious institution, as described above.[105] A *sanad* certifies that an individual has undergone a religious curriculum or is trained and competent in a course, such as Qur'anic studies, *hadith* or Arabic. The last category is reserved for those students who had some level of unspecified or other type of religious education. Recall that this need not involve a religious institution; religious instructors may also come to a parent's home.

- *Length of religious education*: The number of years the militant attended a religious educational institution. Due to the unspecific nature of the information in the biographies we made an assumption that general references made about one's length of religious education were references to the amount of time that individual spent at a madrassa vice some other type of religious institution. If months were mentioned they were converted into years.

- *Nonreligious education*: The highest level of nonreligious education obtained. There were eight possible categories: illiterate; primary (grades one to five); middle (grades six to eight); matriculation (tenth grade); intermediate (grade twelve); graduate (BA or BS); professionals (MA, MS, PhD or other professional degree); or N/A, for data not available. For education obtained at the matric level and above, the militant must have received a degree.

- *Employment:* The employment field is categorized in two ways, a first category consistent with the Pakistani Federal Bureau of Statistics (FBS) data categories, and a second categorization that is customized to this data set. Each of these

---

[105] *Sanad* here refers to a degree obtained at a madrassa. The signification of the *sanad*, such as number of years, courses completed or mastery of a subject, is not discussed in the biographies.

categorizations are self-contained, and in this appendix we call them employment classifications 1 and 2.

Employment classification 1—customized

Employment Categories	Number	Percent	Percent excluding missing
Armed Forces or Police	7	0.8%	2.6%
Farmer	22	2.4%	8.1%
Unskilled Worker	55	5.9%	20.2%
Low-Skilled Worker	82	8.8%	30.1%
White Collar/High Skilled	10	1.1%	3.7%
Teacher	12	1.3%	4.4%
Business or Self-Employed	33	3.6%	12.1%
Unemployed	14	1.5%	5.1%
Government	7	0.8%	2.6%
Other	28	3.0%	10.3%
Religious Leader or Imam	2	0.2%	0.7%
Missing	657	70.7%	

Employment classification 2—FBS Data Consistent

The following are the FBS employment categories. Each observation has been categorized into one of these employment fields.

FBS_Occ_Shopkeeper
FBS_Occ_Personal_business
FBS_Occ_Govt_Servant
FBS_Occ_Pvt_Sector
FBS_Occ_Manual_Laborer_Worker
FBS_Occ_Agriculture
FBS_Occ_Unemployed
FBS_Occ_Professional (Doctor, Lawyer, Engineer, Teacher)
FBS_Occ_Retired
FBS_Occ_HouseholdWoman
FBS_Occ_Armed_forces
FBS_Occ_Other

—In this field, the other category is further subdivided into (a) FBS_Occ_Other_LowSkilled and (b) FBS_OCC_Other_Religious. Thus, a person can be categorized as being "Other" and then also as "Other_Low Skilled."
FBS_Occ_Missing

- *Age upon entry:* The age when the militant was recruited into the organization or carried out basic training. While it can be assumed that these two entry points can be different, the militant's first or earliest exposure to the organization was, when possible, what we coded. This judgment was also based on the assumption that there would not be significant time lapse even if these two incidents were separate. If the age was in a range, the average is reported in the data. For example, the age of 16 to 17 is reported as 16.5.

- *Age at death:* The age at which the militant was killed in battle, oftentimes calculated by subtracting the date of death from year of birth. If the age is in a range, the average is reported in the data.

Residence and Recruitment

- *Hometown:* The name of the village, town or subdistrict as stated in the biography. The spellings for this category and the district and province spellings that follow were standardized according to Pakistan's *Gazetteer*.

- *District:* The district associated with the militant's hometown.

- *Province:* The province associated with the militant's hometown.

- *Means of recruitment:* The means through which the militant was recruited into the group. Based upon our data we were able to identify twelve different channels of LeT recruitment (see below). In a number of cases, multiple means of recruitment were reported. All of these were coded.

Current LeT Member
Family (Father, Brother, Uncle, Cousin, Nephew, Family unspecified, Grandmother)
Mosque
Self-Initiated

Madrassa or Other Islamic Studies Center
Propaganda, Speech or Literature
Friends
Acquaintance not specifically family or friend
LeT Conference
Hizbul Mujahidin Member
LeT Student Wing
Other

Training, Deployment and Death

- *Level of Training*: The highest level of training achieved. In LeT biographies, four main training types exist: training (unspecified), basic training, specialized training and specialized named or other named training. The following categories were thus used to code our data.

  1. Basic Training – when *Daura-e-Aama* was mentioned
  2. Training (Unspecified) – when only the Urdu word for training (*tarbiyat*) was used
  3. Specialized Training – when *Daura-e-Khasa* was mentioned or other Urdu terms for armed training (i.e., *askari tarbiyat*, commando, guerilla) that were used to describe training that had occurred after basic training and that was similar to what is believed to be taught in the *Daura-e-Khasa* course.
  4. Specialized Named or other Named Training – when a specific training name was mentioned that was not *Daura-e-Aama* or *Daura-e-Khasa*.
  5. Training None – when no training was mentioned in the biographies.

The "Specialized Named or other Named Training" category captures several types of trainings. Due to the lack of specific data available about the full range of LeT training courses and their sequencing, the research team was not able to fully differentiate or distinguish between these different types of training (i.e. a course on intelligence collection versus religious training). Since the majority of these trainings are named after companions of the Prophet Muhammad and other historically important figures in Islamic history it is possible that in addition to having physical elements to them many of these courses were also ideological or religious in orientation. Given the lack of specific information about these other named trainings and where they fall in terms of how LeT sequences their training, the research team made an assumption that they followed or complemented *Daura-e-Khasa*. Additional information about the full range and sequencing of LeT training could reveal that some of these named trainings did not follow *Daura-e-Khasa*, but instead preceded it.

- *Length of training:* Length of training in months for the highest level of training obtained. Days and years were converted into months, and ranges are reported in their means.

- *Locations of training:* The stated locations for where a militant trained. If multiple training locations were listed, each was coded.

We created the following categories for training camps' locations.

1. LocTraining_Muzzaffarbad, Pakistan
2. LocTraining_Afghanistan
3. LocTraining_Other
4. LocTraining_Pakistan_or_PakistaniKashmir
5. LocTraining_Missing

Below is the list of all the codes that have been consolidated into each of these categories defined above. The number of observations that fall into each of these categories is in the second column.

Muzaffarabad	Frequency
Afghanistan, Muzaffarabad in Pakistan	1
Abdullah bin Masood	2
Muaskar Abdullah bin Masood	3
Muaskar Abdullah bin Masood in Muzaffarabad	1
Muaskar Afghanistan	1
Muaskar Aqsa, Muzaffarabad	1
Muaskar Umm al-Qura	6
Muaskar Umm al-Qura in Muzaffarabad	1
Muaskar Umm al-Qura, Muzaffarabad	4
Muaskar Umm al-Qura, Pakistan-Kashmir	1
Muaskar, Muzaffarabad	1

Muaskar-e-Taiba in Muzaffarabad	1
Muzaffarabad	30
Muzaffarabad, Pakistan-Kashmir	1
Umm al-Qura	13
Umm al-Qura in Muzaffarabad	4
Umm al-Qura, Muzaffarabad	1

Afghanistan	Frequency
Afghanistan	26
Afghanistan, Muzaffarabad in Pakistan	1
Muaskar Taiba, Afghanistan	1
Muaskar, Afghanistan	1
Muaskar-e-Taiba in Afghanistan	6
Muaskar-e-Taiba, Afghanistan	8

Other	Frequency
Base Camp	5
Muaskar	13
Muaskar Aqsa	2
Muaskar Umm al-Qura in Sanglakh	1
Muaskar-e-Taiba	9
Muaskarat	5
[print cut off]	1

Other Locations in Pakistan	Frequency
Pakistan	2
Pakistan-Kashmir	1

- *Fighting fronts:* The names of countries in which the militant had previously fought. If multiple fronts were mentioned, each was coded.

- *Location of death:* The location where the militant died as stated in the biography. This information was coded at the country, province and district levels. Unless specifically stated, the authors made the assumption that references to Poonch district (it being a district that exists in both India-administered Kashmir and

Pakistan-administered Kashmir) were to Poonch district on the Indian side of the Line of Control.

- *Date of Death:* The date of death as noted in the biography.

APPENDIX B: LIST OF CODED LeT MAGAZINES

The following is a complete list of the fighter biographies that were coded and included in the final version of our original data set.[106]

Hum Ma'en Lashkar-e-Taiba Ki (We, the Mothers of Lashkar-e-Taiba)
181 biographies

- *Hum Ma'en Lashkar-e-Taiba Ki*, Volume 1
- *Hum Ma'en Lashkar-e-Taiba Ki*, Volume 2
- *Hum Ma'en Lashkar-e-Taiba Ki*, Volume 3

Majallah Taibaat (Journal of Virtuous Women)
14 biographies

Year	Issue(s)
2002	January
2003	January, March, July
2004	January, March, April, May, June, August, September

Majallah al-Dawa (Journal for the Call to Islam)
696 biographies

Year	Issue(s)
1994	January, February, May, July, August, October, November
1995	January, February, May, July, August, September, November, December
1996	January, February, April, May, June, July, August, September, October, November, December
1997	January, February, March, April, May, July, August, September, October, November, December
1999	January, February, March, April, May, July, August, October, November, December

---

[106] Note that the research team found several fighter biographies that were repeated across the different LeT publications. All duplicates that the research team could positively identify have been removed and are not reflected in this list.

2000	February, March, April, May, June, June-July, July, August, September, October, November, December
2001	January, February, March, April, June, July, August, September, October, November
2002	February, March, April, May, June, July, August, September, November, December
2003	December
2004	January, February, March, June, July, August, October, November, December
2005	February, March, April, June
2006	August
2007	February, November
—	Undated edition

Mahanah Zarb-e-Taiba (Monthly Strike of the Righteous)

27 biographies

Year	*Issue(s)*
2002	November
2003	September, October, November
2004	January, March, April, June, July, September, October, November, December
2005	January, February, April, May, June

APPENDIX C: PAKISTAN'S POPULATION BY EDUCATIONAL ATTAINMENT LEVEL

(In Percent)

Administrative Unit	Below Primary	Primary	Middle	Matric	Inter-mediate	Diploma/ Certificate	BA/BSc & Equivalent	MA/MSc & Equivalent	Others
Pakistan	18.3	30.14	20.9	17.29	6.56	0.41	4.38	1.58	0.44
Rural	22.57	34.88	20.25	14.71	4.24	0.23	1.96	0.75	0.4
Urban	14.06	25.45	21.54	19.85	8.86	0.58	6.78	2.4	0.48
N W F P	19.78	29.64	19.94	18.61	6.09	0.4	3.43	1.56	0.54
Rural	22.05	31.5	19.74	17.45	4.94	0.29	2.4	1.12	0.5
Urban	13.82	24.75	20.48	21.64	9.11	0.68	6.12	2.74	0.66
Punjab	19.16	31.73	21.81	16.78	5.63	0.32	3.23	1.07	0.28
Rural	22.92	35.65	21.38	14.07	3.6	0.19	1.51	0.44	0.24
Urban	14.58	26.96	22.33	20.09	8.09	0.48	5.33	1.82	0.32
Sindh	15.56	27.13	19.2	17.84	9	0.61	7.43	2.65	0.58
Rural	21.36	36.46	15.19	14.28	6.53	0.34	3.54	1.8	0.51
Urban	13.37	23.61	20.71	19.19	9.93	0.72	8.9	2.97	0.6
Balochistan	19.23	25.91	20.05	18.58	6.48	0.47	4.43	2.37	2.49
Rural	23	28.56	19.44	16.94	4.66	0.33	2.67	1.23	3.17
Urban	15.16	23.06	20.72	20.33	8.43	0.62	6.33	3.59	1.76
Islamabad	14.05	22.68	18.91	17.9	9.84	0.69	10.26	5.24	0.41
Rural	22.46	29.96	22.29	15.45	5.3	0.35	2.88	1.1	0.21
Urban	10.7	19.78	17.56	18.88	11.65	0.83	13.21	6.9	0.49

Source: Pakistan Census Organization, Pakistan Census 1998,

http://www.census.gov.pk/LevelofEducation.htm

APPENDIX D: PROGRAMS OF MADRASSA STUDY AND SECULAR EQUIVALENT

The following table displays programs of Madaris study and their chronological equivalency to non-religious school in Pakistan.

Level	Duration	Certificate (Sanad)	Comparable to Mainstream Education
Nazara	*4 to 5 years*	Shahadatul Tahfeez ul Quran	*Primary (up to 5th grade)*
Hifz-e-Qur'an	*3 years.*	Shahadatul Mutavasatta	*Middle (8th grade)*
Tajveed, Qeeraat	*2 years*	Shahadatul Sanviya ul Amma	*Matric (10th grade)*
Tehtani (Higher secondary)	*2 years*	Shahadatul Sanviya Khasa	Intermediate (FA)
Mohqufaleh Khasa va Sada (College)	*2 years*	Shahadatul Aliya	*BA*
Daura Hadees Sabia va Saniya	*2 years*	Shahadatul Alamiya phil Uluum Arabia vul Islamia	MA and recognized as MA in Arabic and Islamic studies by the Government of Pakistan.

Source: Saleem Mansoor Khalid, ed., *Deeni Madaaris main taaleem* [Education in Religious Schools], (Islamabad: IPS, 2002), 144.